JAN TEUNEN
CHRISTOPH QUARCH
MARTIN HÄUSLER

WHERE THE FUTURE GROWS
CHANGING WORKING ENVIRONMENTS

P. 4
FOREWORD

P. 9
THE GREENHOUSE
THE PHILOSOPHY

P. 51
WISDOM AND FORESIGHT
THE REALITY

P. 213
LEARNING FROM GARDENS
PIET OUDOLF

P. 229
NEIGHBORHOODS FOR THE FUTURE
THE ROLE MODELS

P. 313
HOUSES AS NUTRIENTS
THE VISION

P. 333
PROJECT PARTICIPANTS,
PHOTO CREDITS,
IMPRINT,
INITIATORS

This book is a declaration of love. A declaration of love to the office, the place that has become the hub of our world over the centuries. Day after day, billions of people set off to spend large parts of their lives there. We humans should (and want to) work, drive processes forward, meet key performance indicators, generate great ideas, and, in short, deliver top performance. A lot is demanded of us; that's what we were hired for, and that's what we are paid for. But can we really give our best in an environment that is made available to us for our work, whose design, aesthetics, and energy we are virtually at the mercy of? Can we reach our full potential in offices, these control centers for almost all processes that influence the world, and thus fulfill our responsibility to our company? Or even for our planet? The quality of the work performed determines whether a department, a company, an industry and perhaps even humanity as a whole develops in one direction or the other.

For some time now, job satisfaction figures have shown that employers and employees have become increasingly estranged from one another. All too often, the corporate will to achieve a total increase in efficiency has stood in the way of the human longing for meaning, development, and community. The positive emotional connection with the company—a fundamental prerequisite for productive work—has been lost due to this conflict of interests and has led to a widespread lack of motivation, which is highly damaging in the long term, both for companies and for employees and society.

Therefore, we need to determine what needs to be done to reestablish this connection. We need to ask ourselves what the arguments could be to—on the one hand—reactivate employees who have resigned internally and—on the other—to lure employees who prefer working from home back into the office. Our authors, Jan Teunen and Christoph Quarch, a cultural capital producer and a philosopher, provide these answers. For many years, they have been supporting companies and institutions in their transformations, giving inspiration, impetus, and support for the development of employee potential. The office plays a central role as an essential place of work. In this book, Teunen and Quarch present the essence of what they have distilled from their work and put it up for discussion with key figures in New-Work architecture. To reveal the core of their findings at this point, offices will only be fit for the future if nature finds its way back into their design and becomes an immovable guiding principle. That does not merely mean the greening of workspaces, lounges, and roofs to strengthen the body, mind, and soul of employees and have a direct influence on their mood and health. Instead, it refers to the essence of nature as a blueprint for the character of the office. Nature is a pulsating creative force bursting with vitality, growing, blossoming, bearing fruit, and withering in infinite and countless cycles. It works with symbioses, highly diverse working communities in which billions of “employees” give each other nutrients in order to develop potential and carry life into the future.

However, what could serve as a model for working in the future does not work in a factory where the freedom of nature can hardly be felt because all processes are strictly controlled. But can the other extreme, a wilderness, simply be brought into everyday office life? Jan Teunen and Christoph Quarch, therefore, opted for the metaphor of the garden or the greenhouse—meaningfully and lovingly curated biotopes that offer both protection and freedom—in order to project the foundations of nature into the quarters of the New Work world.

How this can look, how office complexes can be reminiscent of gardens and greenhouses, is also shown by the example of the Lenbachgärten Offices, where this book was created. Munich-based photographer Manfred Jarisch collected impressions for the book. We split these up and placed them between the interview sections. At the same time, journalist and sustainability expert Martin Häusler looks around the world for us with numerous project examples to make it clear that people- and nature-centered office architecture is no longer an exception. On every continent, innovative and creative buildings are emerging that are much more than just workplaces, as they no longer want to be hermetically sealed silos but rather involve their neighborhoods and serve as a source of inspiration for entire districts. In this way, the lost identity is recreated both inside and out.

Flagship projects like these do not emerge from nowhere, nor are they child’s play. Because they undertake the highly complex challenge of bringing yesterday and tomorrow together, they require not only creative visionaries but also bold real estate investors who understand this vision and bring it to life with their financial expertise. Representatives from that sector also have their say in this book.

Finally, let’s not forget that in addition to the urgent update of working environments, the fundamental programming of all trades involved in construction must change. The construction industry generates 60 percent of the world’s waste, and only one percent of the materials used are recycled. Together with the building sector, the construction sector accounts for nearly 40 percent of all energy generated. Cement plants alone are responsible for around eight percent of global carbon dioxide emissions. This makes the industry one of the most significant burdens on our planet—if we also consider the rate at which land is being paved over, which in Germany amounts to 72 soccer pitches per day. The question must be asked: What use is a beautiful house—or a well-designed workplace that people like to visit again, if both were built under unsustainable aspects? Taking nature as our guide means making it the main protagonist in the process of planning and building—or better still, remodeling!—as the main character. That is also the subject of this book. As philosopher Quarch puts it, "new things can only grow where the roots reach deep into the past." And there, at the very beginning, is nature. If I speak of this book as a declaration of love, then this love is first and foremost for her.

Sarah-Joan Fuld

THE GREEN HOUSE

THE GREENHOUSE—Around 200 years ago, the principle of the machine took the place of creative and sustainable creation. Anyone discussing New Work cannot avoid ultimately moving away from this old, technology-based matrix. If you want real change, you need to create workspaces in which the future can flourish. They resemble gardens and greenhouses and thus serve the protected development of potential and co-creation. In this way, entrepreneurs change from producers to curators who nurture and care for life.

WHERE THE FUTURE GROWS. THE PHILOSOPHY—Being human requires a sense of place. Human life, work, business, and housing take place in specific spaces. The design of these spaces is determined by the prevailing economic and lifestyle practices in each cultural area—a particular economy and its associated ethics.

When people's economic and ethical values change, their living and working spaces also change. That is exactly what is happening today. It requires a readjustment of business and life: a visionary view of a new economy and new working environments. More importantly, it requires new guiding principles against which work, its organization, and its housing can be measured.

A new economic model of how we live and work is at the heart of the visionary philosophy of the *Lenbachgärten*: the model of the garden or greenhouse. Office districts of the future will be designed along the lines of gardens. Working environments will resemble greenhouses. The *Lenbachgärten* have the potential to be pioneers and trailblazers of this development. Their vision tells of office spaces that are no longer solely shaped by the imperatives of efficiency and functionality, but by what people need for a fulfilling life. It ventures the utopia of a successful metamorphosis of the working world, in which the gap between life and work is closed and the sterile house of functional value creation is transformed into a blossoming garden of human potential development.

WORLD IN CHANGE. PRESENT—The world of work is changing. Markets are changing, people are changing, and values are changing. Companies are increasingly adopting artificial intelligence and robotics. Machines are taking over activities that people previously carried out. New forms of organization are being tested. Flexible working time models, working from home, and agile management methods are transforming the way some companies operate. At the same time, workplaces are changing. A headline in the *Frankfurter Allgemeine Zeitung* read, "The old office is finally dead." What will take its place is still uncertain. The only certainty is that a lot will change—and that a lot will *need* to change.

A lot needs to change because the number of dissatisfied employees who suffer from their work is constantly increasing. The *Engagement Index*, published annually by the renowned Gallup Institute, stated in 2023 that, "The number of employees without emotional attachment in Germany is at its highest level since 2012." And: "Almost half—45%—of

JAPANESE TRUNK
"For as long as I can remember,
I have been a treasure chest."
Joseph Brodsky

COSMOS

"In my opinion, the cosmos is within us, just as we are within the cosmos. We belong to the universe just as much as it is a part of us."
Yehudi Menuhin

German employees are either actively looking for a new job or are open to new challenges." That will not be without consequences. Gallup estimates that employee dissatisfaction and discontent cost the German economy "between 132.6 and 167.2 billion euros in lost productivity."[1] And that's not all: a survey of German industrial companies conducted by the German Chamber of Industry and Commerce in autumn 2023 revealed that they perceive the shortage of skilled workers as the second-largest current business risk[2]—a concern that has been further fueled by the latest surveys on further declining birth rates and a decreasing willingness of foreign workers to immigrate to Germany. But the challenges continue: while demographic trends mean that fewer and fewer young people are entering the labor market at one end, more and more experienced workers are leaving it at the other—not primarily for health reasons, but due to the desire for more free time:[3] a concern shared by senior citizens and young professionals. In short, the air is getting thin in German companies. Anyone who wants to create the conditions for a successful tomorrow today would do well to invest consistently in employer attractiveness and employee satisfaction. The only question is: how?

The times when employers were able to retain and recruit new employees primarily through monetary incentives are over. Even flexible hours and mobile working options alone are no guarantee of a high level of employer attractiveness. Surveys show that many employees expect their workplace to offer a pleasant working atmosphere, enjoyment, and a sense of purpose in addition to the factors mentioned above.[4] It is also important for them that their employer consistently fulfills its social responsibility and credibly represents values they can identify with.

All these trends point in the same direction: the economic success of organizations in the future will depend to a large extent on whether they succeed in generating an attractive corporate culture that convincingly serves the lifestyle and expectations of employees. That will only succeed if companies have the courage to fundamentally change; and that means not just making a few cosmetic corrections, but disruptively and consistently moving away from the mindset of optimization, functionality, tools, and skills—from economic rationality. The easiest way to illustrate this concept is to look at the image of a machine. A machine serves to subject given resources to a value creation process. The more efficient, functional, and productive the machine is—and the higher the yield—the better. Accordingly, entrepreneurs and managers view themselves as engineers, whose primary task is to optimize the machine's functionality and maximize output in the long term. The only problem is that you can maintain a machine with this technical-instrumental mindset, but you cannot cultivate a corporate culture. For the latter, you need a different way of thinking, a different mental matrix that also brings emotional, communicative, and social skills to bear. In short, the mental paradigm implemented in the minds of many managers and entrepreneurs today is unsuitable for creating the conditions for future economic success. And that is a problem.

This problem can also be described as follows: The economic rationality of the machine matrix has unleashed considerable monetary and material growth over the last 50 years, but at the same time has neglected human growth.

This has consequences for companies. As long as they follow the machine matrix, they cannot possibly become places where people feel comfortable. Today's office buildings are often far from nourishing and energizing the souls of those who work there. They are not made for creativity and *joie de vivre*. All this leads to extraordinary frictional losses in society and companies, generating immense economic damage in the long term.

It doesn't have to stop there. An intellectual paradigm shift in economic activity is not only necessary, but also possible. The history of the economy teaches us that there have always been transformations and mutations in its course, and that new ideas, perspectives, and visions have always triggered these changes. This, it seems, was usually the case when people looked both forwards and backwards in times of upheaval and crisis: when they reassured themselves of their cultural origins and their evolved identity in order to shape the future inspired by them. Or to put it figuratively: if they had the courage to sail with the spirit blowing from the past and—carried by it—set sail for new shores. When people are gripped and moved by a good spirit in this way, we refer to it as enthusiasm. Enthusiasm is the energy of life-giving change. Sparking enthusiasm is the task facing companies and organizations today if they want to be successful tomorrow. They will succeed if they have the courage to open themselves up to the dimension of the spirit, to think differently, accept new paradigms and parameters, and redefine the idea and meaning of doing business. The future is open. It is up to us to shape it.

EARTH

"Everything comes from an egg; and our globe is a large egg which contains all the others."
Voltaire

NATURE

"Everything that comes from Nature's hand is good."
Johann Wolfgang von Goethe

MEMORY—A long memory is necessary for authentic, profound, and sustainable change processes. One must go far back into the past to gain the momentum for a leap that will usher in a genuinely new, different, and positive future. Creativity draws its disruptive energy from memory. As the ancient Greeks already knew, *Mnēmosynē*—memory—is the mother of the nine muses, whose creative spirit not only invigorates and inspires people but also opens new horizons for thought. Therefore, we turn back to history to ask: What should we remember *today* to create new office spaces *tomorrow*?

It is no coincidence that there are nine fragments of memory that we desire to lift from the bosom of the past and bring to our consciousness.

1. Cosmos—The first memory is that of the cosmos: the greater whole, which the ancient Romans called the *universe*—the *inward-looking-one*—for which the German language has the word *All* and for which the English language has the word *Space*.

The Greek word *kósmos* says even more, however. It testifies to an awareness of the world that senses a beautiful order in everything. *Kósmos* originally meant adornment, splendor, or beauty. Our word *cosmetics* is derived from *kósmein—to decorate, to order*. As the beautiful order of all things, all life, and all movement, the cosmos was—in the Greeks' imagination—essential and influential for human life. Just as everything in the cosmos is interconnected, everything interlocks, and everything plays together, it was also important to organize one's own life, economy, or society in the same manner: in such a way that everything harmonizes with each other, agrees with itself and accords with the great cycles of nature. Such a coherent world that fits into its environment should also be the future of office spaces—small, beautiful, coherent, and well-ordered living systems: microcosms that reflect the order of our universe.

2. Earth—We remember our solid, wide home—the "broad-breasted Earth," as *Hesiod* (in the 8th century BCE) loved to call our home planet:[5] the "strong foundation," who "feeds everything in the world," to use the words of the poet behind the *Homeric Hymns* once again.[6] Modern science speaks of it more soberly. It tells us that the Earth has been orbiting the sun for 4.6 billion years and has been populated by living beings for 3.6 billion years; for the past 100,000 years, that has included humans, too. These figures underscore that the Whole was not created for us and that we share our home planet with other species. They admonish us to be humble and remind us that we are not, as the philosopher

“I THINK BUILDINGS SHOULD IMITATE ECOLOGICAL SYSTEMS.”
KEN YEANG

René Descartes (1596–1650) demanded, “lords and masters of nature.”[7] In fact, we are temporary passengers on a wonderful living spaceship, which we must preserve and protect.

3. Nature—Furthermore, we commemorate nature, or more precisely *physis*, as it was conceived in ancient Greece: not as a sphere of objects that differ from all others in that they are not made by human hands, but have grown of their own accord—as the wonderful, both chaotic and orderly event that constantly produces new individual beings and yet remains bound by eternal laws. In everything, *physis* follows its incorruptible and consistent logic. Nature is simultaneously wasteful and efficient, destructive and creative, changeable and permanent. In everything, it seeks to develop its inherent potential fully.

In this, it is created for both functionality and beauty. Wherever it comes fully into its own, it shows itself in full bloom and bears rich fruit. It is always concerned with developing and fulfilling life.

If we set out to consistently orient ourselves towards nature with all our skill and ability—for instance, in the area of architecture and the interior design of future office spaces—failure is almost impossible.

4. Human—The origin of European culture is condensed in just two words: *Gnōthi sauton—Know thyself!* These were the words of an inscription in the porch of the Temple of Apollo at Delphi, the central shrine of ancient Greece. These words were not an appeal to navel-gazing and psychoanalysis, but to reflect on what it means to be human. What does it mean to be human? This is how the women and men of antiquity saw themselves questioned by their god, and this is how the first philosophers of our tradition asked. One of their answers is that all people are concerned with the good life. All people long for meaning. Only when we recognize meaning in our lives and in our world will we achieve true happiness. The most important ingredients for this are two experiences that we have already had in the womb: the intimate connection with something else that is greater than us—and the freedom to be able to develop into an individual self; and this in a holistic sense: physically, rationally, emotionally and spiritually—as body, as ego, as soul and as spirit. Freedom and connectedness in these four dimensions are the basic qualities of a successful human being. And the energy that inspires us to do this was honored by our ancestors in ancient Greece as the passionate love of Eros.

5. House—Let us continue to remember how we became sedentary. The house is a late invention in human history. The first house was probably built sometime after the last ice age, around 12,000 years ago. The Roman architect *Vitruvius* (born around 75 BCE) described the process in vivid images. In his work *Ten Books on Architecture*, he tells us that in prehistoric times, humans lived like wild animals in forests, caves, and groves.[8] One day, however, a fire broke out in a dense jungle as a result of a lightning strike. The people fled from the flames, but when the fire finally died down, they curiously crawled out of their hiding places, went to the scene, and stepped into a clearing created by the fire. They stayed there, experienced themselves as a community, and gradually began to develop a language. Now they started to build huts—a skill they perfected over time, until "by daily activity, they had made their hands more skilled in building houses, and by skill and exercise of mind had brought it beyond the conventional process to a skill of art." [9] This story reveals something about the meaning of the art of building: the mastery of architecture consists in giving people a space in which they can live humanely. That is always possible when a house combines five practical elements: (1) It provides protection and security for its residents. (2) It opens up a space for togetherness or sociability. (3) It gives people a sense of home and a sense of identity. (4) It allows residents to educate themselves and cultivate their culture. (5) It enables them to work and do business. Where a house incorporates these five aspects, it becomes a *home*—a place where we can work and live humanely.

6. Oikonomía—The ancient economy was in many ways different from today's global economic system of capitalism and liberalism. Its name, *oikonomía*, reveals the spirit that guided economic activity in ancient Greece: it is comprised of the words *oíkos*, meaning "house," and *nomía*, meaning "order." Originally, *oikonomía* was nothing more than *the order of the house*: the set of rules by which a house could be organized and managed. But what should determine who was responsible for a house? *Vitruvius* also provides an original answer to this question: before they built houses, people had lived outdoors. Every night, they gazed up at the sky and marveled at the wonderful structure of the cosmos, which seemed perfectly harmonious and coherent to them. This provided them with a model for economic activity: The *oikonomía* should correspond to the basic order of nature and fit into the great harmony of life. This idea can also be found in the oldest theoretical reflection on economics in European culture. It can be found in the first book of Politics, from Aristotle

HUMAN

"Humans must construct meaning.
That is the beauty and our consolation."
Stephen J. Gould

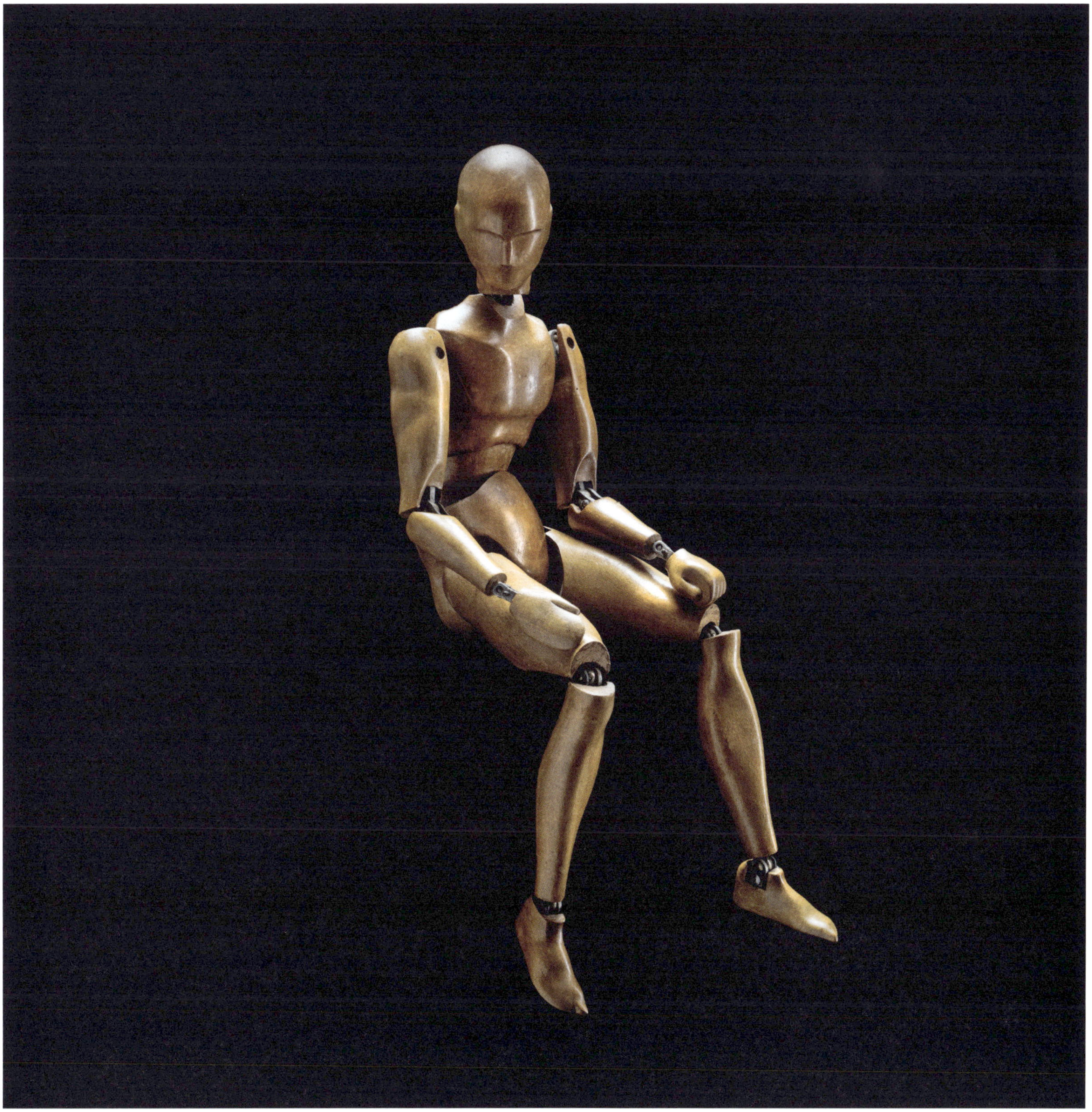

HOUSE
"With mutual trust one can build a tidy little house."
Johann Wolfgang von Goethe

(384–322 BCE). In it, the philosopher asks: How is the success of the *oíkos* measured? How does *oikonomía* succeed? His answers are still worth considering: the purpose of economic activity is to enable people who work and live together in a house to lead a good life, a free life without dependencies, which makes it possible to participate as citizens in the democratic administration and government of the polis and at the same time to find the time and space for what makes people human: culture, sociability, identity. According to *Aristotle*, economics has the task of ensuring the independence of the *oíkos*. The economist's goal was *autárkeia*, the *self-sufficiency of the house*, which consisted in the fact that it could produce everything of its own accord or had the necessary resources for everything that people needed for their livelihood—food, shelter, hygiene, energy, etc.—and which created the conditions for them to be able to pursue their public and private affairs in freedom. Economic success is measured by whether a company provides all its members with a space in which they can live a dignified, fear-free, safe, sociable, cultivated, natural—in short, a good life. The purpose of business, as *Aristotle* believed, is not profit or mere living, but the good life in freedom and community, in harmony with the living being.

7. Cloister—Our journey down memory lane takes us back to the Middle Ages, or more precisely, to the world of monasteries. The ideal of the ancient economy lives on in them to this day. *Benedict of Nursia* (480–547) wrote in his Rule that every abbey had to be self-sufficient so that its inhabitants could pursue what they considered desirable: a spiritual, contemplative, consecrated life. The motto of monastic management was not to *generate as much income as possible in the shortest time possible*, but to ensure stability and longevity while guaranteeing the living space for a good life. This is why the abbeys were to be completely autonomous and independent. They should therefore be in a position to produce all the goods necessary for their livelihood themselves. With this in mind, it is hardly surprising that the office was invented in the monasteries during the High Middle Ages. The word "bureau" is derived from the "burra," the *monk's robe*, which pious men spread out on their writing desks in the scriptorium to protect the precious books. The protection of the precious has been the very idea of the office ever since. It is still important to preserve it today. Only in times of digitalization and artificial intelligence is it no longer books that are precious and in need of protection, but the people who do their work in the office.

8. Renaissance—The Renaissance was an era in which people freed themselves from the grip of religion and revived the spirit of antiquity. A new attitude to life spread, which led to the unification of three previously separate areas of life: Science, economics, and art. The scholars of the time developed humanism, the *entrepreneurs* an early form of capitalism, and the artists a new aesthetic based on antiquity. This also changed the model of economic activity. A new type of merchant emerged: the *entrepreneur*. In his *Essai sur la Nature du Commerce au Général* (1755), *Richard Cantillon* (1680–1734) describes him as a person who acquires or produces something at a certain price to resell it at a higher price at a later date. The *entrepreneur* now appears as a venturer who sets off for new shores in order to return home richly laden from afar. His goal is a return on investment to use the capital for new investments. He makes a pact with the future, and the house that is of use to him can float. It is a ship, with which he overcomes the spatial and temporal limits imposed on the old economy. Growth is decoupled from nature. Technology takes its place: a technology that increases ability; that makes people wealthy in both senses of the word; that transforms everything natural into resources.

9. Machine—Our last memory is of the 18th and 19th centuries. Once again, business is changing. The *entrepreneur* becomes sedentary. He becomes an industrialist who replaces the ship with apparatuses and machines as an instrument of value creation. Technology is now fully put at the service of industry: Factories sprout up like mushrooms. They are fueled by a new mindset that we can call the *machine matrix*: Resources—whether *monetary, material, human, or data resources*—are processed through ever more efficient, functional, productive value creation procedures to generate optimal output (as goods, money, wealth, power, etc.). The imperative of this new form of economy is: ever faster, ever more, ever more efficient, ever more productive, ever more functional. The entrepreneur is no longer a *venturer* who steers his ship boldly into a hopeful future, but a machinist who maintains the machine in sweaty overalls. Ancient economics focused on the good life, while modern economics emphasizes wealth. And that in a double sense. It is about the accumulation of capital—*financial assets*—in order to do many things with its help, in the sense of being able to do things or making things possible. As the goal of economic activity, *wealth* has taken the place of *property*, *ability* has taken the place of *being*, and *being able to do a lot* (or *power*) has taken the place of *being good*. This corresponds to a profound shift in the

OIKONOMIA

"The word oikonomia dates back to the time of Pericles (500/490–429 BCE) and is used to describe the sensible management of all matters relating to the household of a free citizen."
Horst Meyer

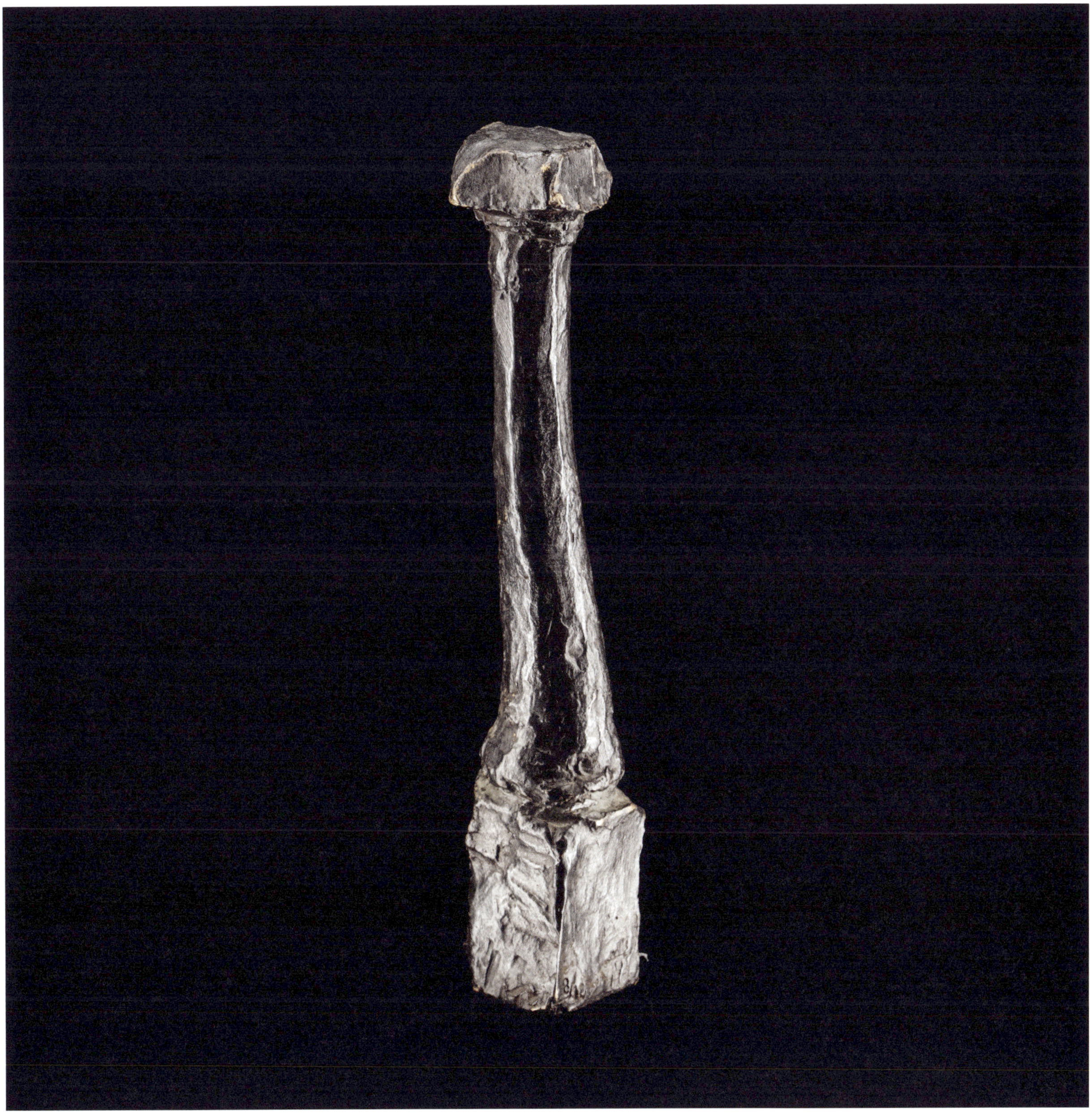

MONASTERY

"The office was invented in a monastery during the High Middle Ages. It was expressly developed to preserve and protect precious items and to invent new treasures continually."
Hajo Eickhoff

perception of time. Under the influence of modern economics, people have forgotten how to dwell in the present. They are always ahead of themselves and their time. Instead of anchoring themselves in the here and now, they settle in a future they desire. They promise themselves success, happiness, and wealth from what *could be*, not from what *is*.

As a result, their lives are becoming increasingly complex. To keep pace, they have begun to fragment their living environment. To maintain their overview, they have exchanged the simple for the complex. Now they can no longer find an end because the beginning has been lost. As a result, office districts no longer work today. Permeated by the machine matrix, the houses of work have been transformed into machines. With the result that you can no longer live in them: They provide no protection, they are not cultural spaces, they are not meeting places, they do not create a home. They are purely functional spaces that follow the imperatives of technical rationality. This is why people are fleeing: into inner resignation, into illness, into drugs ... They hope to be saved by a better *work-life balance*, but this remains an illusion as they have turned themselves into machines and sacrificed their "free time" to the imperatives of economic rationality. Whether as entrepreneurs of their own lives, as self-marketers in the digital market of the attention economy, or as consumers, people are converting themselves into commodities, wealthy perhaps, but steadily losing their being and identity in the process.

As long as the machine matrix determines economic activity, today's widespread calls for *New Work, Workshift*, or a better *work-life balance* will not bring about any real change. At best, new methods and technologies will optimize the functionality of the machine and the machine-like people one last time, before the machine has completely overheated and collapses.

If you want change, you shouldn't be satisfied with turning a few screws on an increasingly dysfunctional machine. Those who want change are well advised to leave behind technical thinking and break free from the machine-driven matrix of today's economy. Those who want change will create spaces where the future can grow. They will resemble gardens: places where people can live.

THE GARDEN OF THE FUTURE—The future will grow if we succeed in no longer organizing the economy according to machine logic, but rather according to the guiding metaphor of a garden. Gardens are places of life. They are not production sites. It is not the making that gives gardens their character, but the culture—the nurturing and care of the living things that are allowed to germinate, grow, blossom, and flourish within them. That is why a gardener is something different from the modern-day *venturer* or entrepreneur who makes a pact with the future in which he invests. For the gardener, the future is not a commodity with which he can trade. He lives in the present, where he cultivates his property. He cultivates the space in which the future can grow and life can unfold.

1. Development—What are gardens? You can visualize their place in the spiritual topography of life when you think of medieval towns: there is the town surrounded by a wall, with artisans' workshops, stores, and churches clustered around the market square. Around the city wall is a belt of gardens. This is where the townspeople cultivate their flowers and vegetables. And beyond the gardens, the open countryside, nature, and the wilderness open up. Gardens are intermediate spaces. They are situated between the city, which is shaped by human activity, wealth, and economic activity, and the wilderness, which lies beyond human control. Gardens are in-between spaces in which man cultivates nature, which is unavailable to him.

2. Beauty—What human needs does a garden satisfy? It is tempting to answer that the requirements of physical well-being are met, and to refer to orchards, vineyards, vegetable gardens, herb gardens, and other *kitchen gardens*. However, this falls short. A garden is always *also*, but never *only*, a kitchen garden. A pure kitchen garden would be a *plantation* or a *nursery*, but not a garden. A garden not only serves people's physical needs, but also their spiritual and mental well-being. That is why there are not only kitchen gardens, but also pleasure or ornamental gardens. Gardens combine aesthetics and functionality, art and efficiency, beauty and usefulness. Gardens nourish people in all dimensions of their lives: not only physically with fruit and vegetables, but also mentally and spiritually with beauty and poetry. European literature is therefore full of descriptions of beautiful gardens. One motif that persists is that of the *locus amoenus* (Latin for a *lovely place*). This was understood to mean a particularly appealing and inviting place in nature, which typically included birdsong and flowers, as well as a light-filled grove, a spring, or a stream. Early medieval authors such as *Isidore of Seville* (c. 560–636) and *Rabanus Maurus* (780–856) explicitly define the *locus amoenus* in their works as a place that is not used for commercial purposes but is used solely for pleasure and love.

3. Art—As cultural spaces that combine beauty and utility, aesthetics and functionality, gardens are always also places of art. Not only because people have tended to decorate their gardens with sculptures, artistic water features, or other arrangements since the days of antiquity, but also because gardens are themselves works of art in an emphatic sense—works of art that appeal equally to all the senses and therefore touch people holistically. "We see, hear, smell, we can taste fruit, we can feel the wind and sun on our skin. We are just as exposed to the weather and atmospheric moods as we are to the effects that a garden designer has created for us," writes garden philosopher *Hans von Trotha* (born 1965) in his book *Der romantische Garten*.[10] No one else has formulated the resulting task of specific garden design as aptly as *Friedrich Schiller* (1759–1805). In his essay *Ueber den Gartenkalender auf das Jahr 1795*, he notes that the aim of horticulture must be to "enhance the enjoyment of life that contact with beautiful natural landscapes can give us."[11] Increasing the "enjoyment of life" or liveliness: This is indeed what we get from an artistically designed, beautiful garden. The more artistically designed the garden is, the more alive and vital we feel within it. Perhaps this is the reason why there has always been a close connection between gardens and eroticism in European culture. In ancient Greece, there were sacred gardens dedicated to the goddess Aphrodite, reserved for human sensual pleasures—a motif that recurred in the Baroque and Rococo periods, when garden architects competed to include "Islands of Venus" or "Grottos of Venus" in their garden designs. The philosopher *Plato* (428/427–348/347 BCE) already recounted that the god Eros, so important to the Greeks, was conceived in a garden—a point that can only be truly understood when one considers that in Greek thought, Eros was understood not merely in a sexual sense, but as the fundamental principle of vitality that pervades all dimensions of human life. For the Greeks, Eros was the driving force behind the development of all potential. He is nourished and inspired by beauty. Therefore, it's understandable that he feels at home nowhere more than in a beautiful garden, where everything sprouts and blooms, where everything grows and bears fruit.

4. Growth—Gardens are not only places of beauty, art and eroticism, but usually also places of value creation and growth—not only material and monetary growth, but also human and cultural growth, a natural, cyclical growth that, unlike unnatural, exponential growth, is not dominated by the machine matrix of the modern economy. The growth of a garden is not limitless. It finds its double limit in the possibilities of the nature cultivated in the garden and in the requirements of the people who cultivate it. People benefit from the produce of the garden. What they cannot use directly is returned to it as humus and fertilizer. This creates a sustainable, natural circular economy—an economy tied back to the great cycles of nature. This is where gardening differs from a machine economy. At the same time, gardeners certainly appreciate its advantages. This is why the plea for an economy based on the garden does not imply a rejection of technology and machines. Technical equipment will also be used in an economy based on the garden metaphor. Only the priorities change. In gardening, technology is put at the service of life, and life is not used to operate technical devices.

5. Humanity—Gardens are humane economic spaces: spaces of a humane, natural, largely self-sufficient, and sustainable economy. They are spaces of moderate growth that take the good life as a measure—a good life that does not wait for people beyond the garden after work, but that can be celebrated while they are working in it: because gardens are sometimes ornamental gardens whose layout and floral splendor give people pleasure; because they invite people to linger; because people can be creative and expressive in them. The reason why people love gardens and enjoy spending time in them is the combination of functionality and aesthetics. In a garden, people are surrounded by life and culture. Here, they are connected back to nature and can live in accordance with it. Here, they can cultivate and thrive.

6. Sociability—Gardens provide space for human interaction. They are places that provide people as social and creative beings with a worthy place to stay. European cultural history also bears witness to this impressively. It is therefore no coincidence that the great schools of philosophy in antiquity were often located in gardens. For instance, *Plato* founded his Academy in the 4th century BCE, in a sacred grove dedicated to the muses outside the gates of Athens. *Epicurus* (around 341–271/270 BCE) followed his example almost two centuries later and also acquired a garden as the seat of the community he initiated. Here, as there, not only was scientific research carried out. Social life and the exchange of ideas between residents at symposia and games were a central pillar of these communities—an ideal that was later followed by the *Nuova Academia*, founded by *Marsilio Ficino* (1433–1499) in the garden villa Careggi near Florence, which quickly developed into an intellectual epi-

NUMBERS 3 AND 4

"People who lead in this way ensure that all four dimensions of the human being are addressed in the working environment:
1. Body
2. Self
3. Mind
4. Soul"
John Nisberg

SAILING SHIP

"If you wish to build a ship, do not divide the men into teams and send them to the forest to cut wood. Instead, teach them to long for the vast and endless sea."
Antoine de Saint-Exupéry

center of the Renaissance. Probably the most famous literary description of a social gathering in European literature dates from this period: The *Decameron*, by *Giovanni Boccaccio* (1313–1375). The author tells the story of a group of young aristocrats who spend a few days together in a villa outside the gates of Florence to escape the plague raging in the city. The garden of this villa becomes the setting for a humanistic way of life dedicated entirely to the good, the true, and the beautiful, whose cheerfulness and vitality speak for centuries from *Boccaccio's* lines: "The aspect of this garden, its fair order, the plants and the fountain and the rivulets that flowed from it, so charmed the ladies and the three young men that with one accord they affirmed that they knew not how it could receive any accession of beauty, or what other form could be given to Paradise, if it were to be planted on earth. [...] At length, however, they had enough of wandering about the garden and observing this thing and that: wherefore they repaired to the beautiful fountain, around which were ranged the tables, and there, after they had sung half-a-dozen songs and trod some measures, they sat them down, at the queen's command, to breakfast, which was served with all celerity and in fair and orderly manner, the viands being both good and delicate; whereby their spirits rose, and up they got, and betook themselves again to music and song and dance, and so sped the hours [...]." [12] In this description, conviviality, nature, and beauty combine to create a celebration of humanity and joie de vivre, for which there is no better setting than an artfully-landscaped garden. A beautiful garden supports people in developing their sociable and social nature, allowing them to interact with one another in a meaningful way.

7. Co-Creation—Gardens are spaces of co-creation. Not only insofar as they inspire the human intellect to develop productive cultivation methods, not only insofar as they nourish the human soul with their beauty, but above all insofar as the co-creative spirit of living nature reigns in gardens. This is precisely what is evident in a garden: its economic prosperity and aesthetic beauty are due to the fact that there is constant creative interaction taking place within it. Plants interact with each other, plants interact with animals, and animals interact with each other—everything interacts with air and sunlight, wind and rain. The garden is a complex living system that constantly generates new life by fertilizing each other. Clever gardeners know how to make use of this creative dynamic. The horticultural methods of permaculture or regenerative agriculture, for example, see themselves as an art of composition whose mastery lies in strengthening and supporting the living interaction of the garden in such a way that gardeners can achieve a maximum yield with a minimum of effort. A rich harvest with little effort—and in a completely natural way. Astonishingly, a very economically successful German DIY chain has turned the unspoken mantra of permaculture into a popular advertising slogan: “Let nature do its thing!”

8. Harmony—Gardens are living systems. To manage them successfully, you must be able to think systematically. This requires being able to focus on both the individual plant and the garden as a whole. After all, a living system is only healthy if the individual parts interacting within it can assert themselves in their particularity and uniqueness without hindering or blocking their fellow players, and in a way that integrates all participants into a coherent whole. Our ancestors in ancient Greece referred to this basic systemic principle as *harmonía*. They did not understand it to mean a harmonious or tensionless coexistence, but, on the contrary, a tense interaction in which antagonistic forces are not eliminated or neutralized, but rather synergistically related to one another. Harmonic systems resemble musical compositions that do not captivate through their monotony, but through their dynamic, multifaceted, yet coherent complexity. Just as a living garden inspires us because the dynamic complexity of life is staged within it in such a way that we can understand it and be reflected in it. A beautiful garden is like a tuning fork: it invites us to resonate with it and to harmonize with and enhance our own complex vitality.

9. Protection—Living systems are fragile. That is why gardens, by their very nature and origin, are protected places. Their name reveals this. The word garden is derived from *gerte* (Indo-European *gher* or *ghortos*). This refers to willow, hazelnut rods, or other types of wood that were interwoven to enclose the garden near the house, protecting it from wild animals. The walled garden, known as the *hortus conclusus*, can be found as early as *Homer*, as well as in the Middle Ages. Here, the etymology refers to the Indo-European word *cart* (*protection*), which lives on in the French *jardin* (*garden*) as well as in the English *yard* (*courtyard*), the Scandinavian *gaard* (*farmstead*), or the Slavic *grad* (*castle*). Even the most famous of all gardens, paradise, reveals with its name the original character of the garden as an enclosed place, as the ancient Iranian *pairi-dae'za* means nothing other than *enclosure*. Gardens are protected, clearly demarcated places. Above all, they are separated from the world of everyday activity with its economic constraints. The fenced, walled, and enclosed garden is a different world. It does not claim to be a place where people

THE GOLDEN BOAT

"The civilization of ancient Greece was nurtured within city walls. In fact, all the modern civilizations have their cradles of brick and mortar. These walls leave their mark deep in the minds of men. They set up a principle of 'divide and rule' in our mental outlook, which begets in us a habit of securing all our conquests by fortifying them and separating them from one another. We divide nation and nation, knowledge and knowledge, man and nature. It breeds in us a strong suspicion of whatever is beyond the barriers we have built, and everything has to fight hard for its entrance into our recognition."
Rabindranath Tagore

VITRUVIUS

"Architecture is generated by people's needs, both spiritual and material. It has a lot to do with optimism, joy, and a sense of security. It attempts to bring order to a disordered world, to give people privacy amid the hustle and bustle, and to create space even in the smallest of places. And to bring light on a gloomy day."
Lord Norman Foster

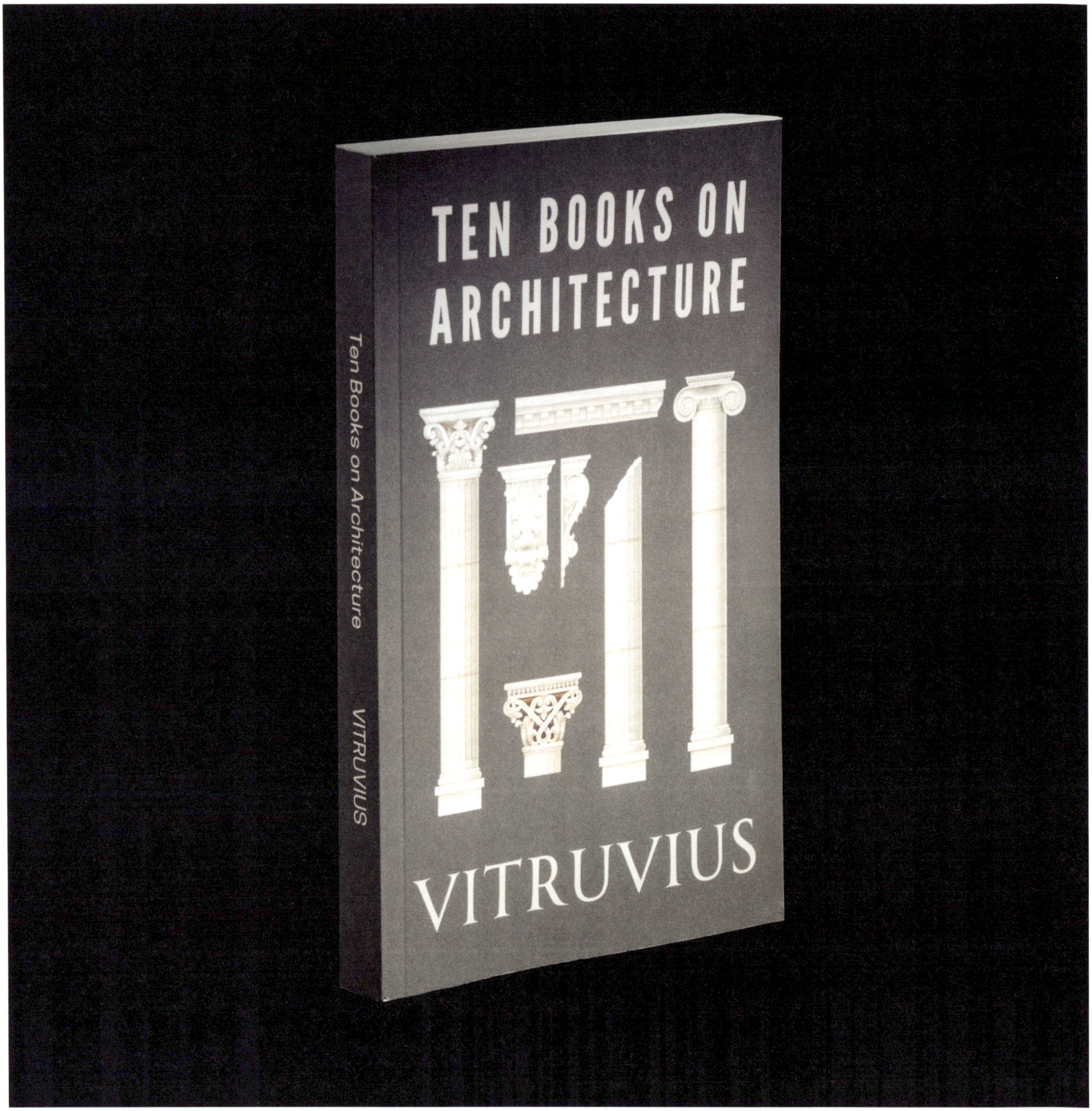

can live and work. Perhaps this is why no one has ever considered making it the guiding metaphor for economic activity, especially since it is open at the top, allowing people within it to be exposed to the forces of nature. The fact that this is an advantage only becomes clear at a time when man has become alienated from nature: As an open cultural space, the garden remains close to nature. Unlike in the machine halls and houses of the modern economy, the connection to the cosmos is maintained in the garden.

But does the garden, which opens to the sky as a model of economic activity, not harbor too many risks? Does the economy not need a protective roof over its head? Does a successful combination of economy and work not require a solid house, and an order or *oikonomía* that is appropriate to the solid house? Yet who is to say that life and economic activity in accordance with gardens would not be possible in a house—that a new *oikonomía* could not be located in a different kind of *oíkos*? The metaphor is ready and waiting: the greenhouse.

THE GREENHOUSE. VISION—The roofed garden is the visionary guiding metaphor for future office spaces. It draws on the economy of antiquity to combine it with modern entrepreneurship. From antiquity, it has adopted the qualities of naturalness, self-sufficiency, and humanity, as well as an orientation toward the five traditional basic functions of the house (*oikos*).[13] From modern entrepreneurship, this guiding metaphor inherits the dynamics of stable and consistent growth. It succeeds in making this connection because it takes the art of gardening as its yardstick and translates it into a sustainable economy. Metaphorically speaking, its home is no longer a machine hall, but a greenhouse.

To avoid any possible misunderstandings, it is first necessary to distinguish between a *greenhouse* and a *hothouse*. A greenhouse is a roofed garden; a hothouse is a roofed plantation. Greenhouses are found wherever economic rationality prevails. In them, plant growth is optimized and the yield maximized. The hothouse follows the stringency of the machine. The greenhouse, on the other hand, is not a pure production facility. What is it then? Again, nine aspects allow us to recognize the essence of the greenhouse.

1. Culture—A greenhouse is a place where life is *cultivated*—a place of good living. It is a place where plants find the optimum climate to grow and thrive, and where they are supplied with all the nutrients they need. The atmosphere of the greenhouse is adapted to the plants being cultivated. The roofing allows the incidence of light, temperature, and

“RESHAPE ENVIRONMENT; DON’T TRY TO RESHAPE MAN.”
R. BUCKMINSTER FULLER

humidity to be varied independently of external conditions, thereby simulating a natural environment. In this way, life in the greenhouse remains tied back to the great cycles of nature. It fits into the great web of life. The symbol of this is the glass roof: the stars that give direction to earthly life are still visible from inside the house. Growth and prosperity follow the principles of life and are not forcibly imposed by technology. This does not mean that technical aids are not used in it. On the contrary: AI-controlled air-conditioning technology, regeneratively generated energy, and subtle irrigation techniques—all of this can and should be in the greenhouse, but in the service of natural and sustainable growth.

2. Sustainability—Ideally, a greenhouse is self-sufficient. Making clever use of sunlight can largely eliminate the need for an external energy supply. Any additional energy required can be generated from renewable sources. Canals and cisterns based on ancient aqueducts supply the greenhouse with water. Humus and fertilizer are obtained through composting. This is recycling management at its best. By guaranteeing the security of resources in this way, an office area managed according to greenhouse standards can achieve maximum freedom and independence, much like a medieval abbey, and thus keep its value creation free from disruptive influences. Extensive self-sufficiency and sustainability make the greenhouse a place of lasting and reliable prosperity.

3. Humanity—In a greenhouse, people take center stage. Because they gain guidance for their lives from their connection to nature, they no longer experience their work as something alienating, but as something true to their nature. Here they will find an atmosphere conducive to their personal growth and an invigorating climate. Everything that nourishes them in body, soul, and spirit is available: healthy conditions that are good for their bodies, an aesthetically pleasing environment that puts them in a good mood, and an inspiring culture that constantly inspires them anew. Perhaps also a management approach based on the art of gardening, which makes it its mission to encourage people in their personal growth. In the spirit of the British entrepreneur *Richard Branson* (born in 1950), who once said, "people are no different from flowers. If you water them, they flourish. If you are not nice to them, they shrivel up."

4. Security—A greenhouse is a protected yet open space where people can lead a healthy life, both physically and mentally, and feel safe at the same time. This sense of security is not only due to the physical protection provided by the walls and roof, but above all to the fact that people are reliably supplied with everything they need to live and work well: physically, mentally, and spiritually. In this way, humane office areas are created in the true sense of the word, which simultaneously satisfy the needs of people and the conditions of nature, providing protected areas where people can co-creatively and innovatively develop their potential.

5. Transparency—A greenhouse is open to the sky and the world. Its glass walls allow a lively exchange with its surroundings. It enables those who work in it to stay informed about global developments, adapt to changing times, and find the right solutions to emerging challenges. In this way, they can keep pace with developments in the market, nature, and technology. In this way, office areas organized according to the greenhouse model remain connected to society. The companies of the future will need to have an open, honest, and transparent exchange with society. The time when they could hide behind walls and masks is over. In the new economy, compliance is a matter of course. People's trust is the most precious capital and the highest value of future companies. Their value creation will not only focus on monetary values, but also increasingly on ethical values such as trust, reliability, and honesty.

6. Community—The greenhouse is a place with light transparency and honesty. There is nothing to hide; communication is open. There is a culture of mindfulness, appreciation, and tolerance. This is how trust can grow: the *humus of all cooperation*. Where there is trust, people can rely on each other and treat each other without fear. It is a truism that those who sit in glass houses should not throw stones. What is even more important is the principle of mutual support, which has been copied from horticulture—namely, permaculture: everyone in the greenhouse promotes the growth of others through their actions. Cooperation, togetherness, and team spirit flourish in open meeting spaces where people can engage in conversation beyond their routines and objectives: park benches and lawns, clearings, and outdoor seating, to stay with the garden metaphor. Translated into the world of tomorrow's office districts, we envision lounges, cafés, or actual garden areas where togetherness can flourish.

7. Individuality—Greenhouses foster an environment in which creativity flourishes. People become creative in spaces that offer two things: free, informal, and open meeting places, as well as quiet, private retreats. Just as a greenhouse provides the light, partial shade

BRAIN

"The world most people grow up in is one that has been shaped, more or less consciously, by the standards of previous generations. This is not necessarily a particularly humane world, and therefore not necessarily a world in which optimal conditions for the development of the human brain prevail."
Gerald Hüther

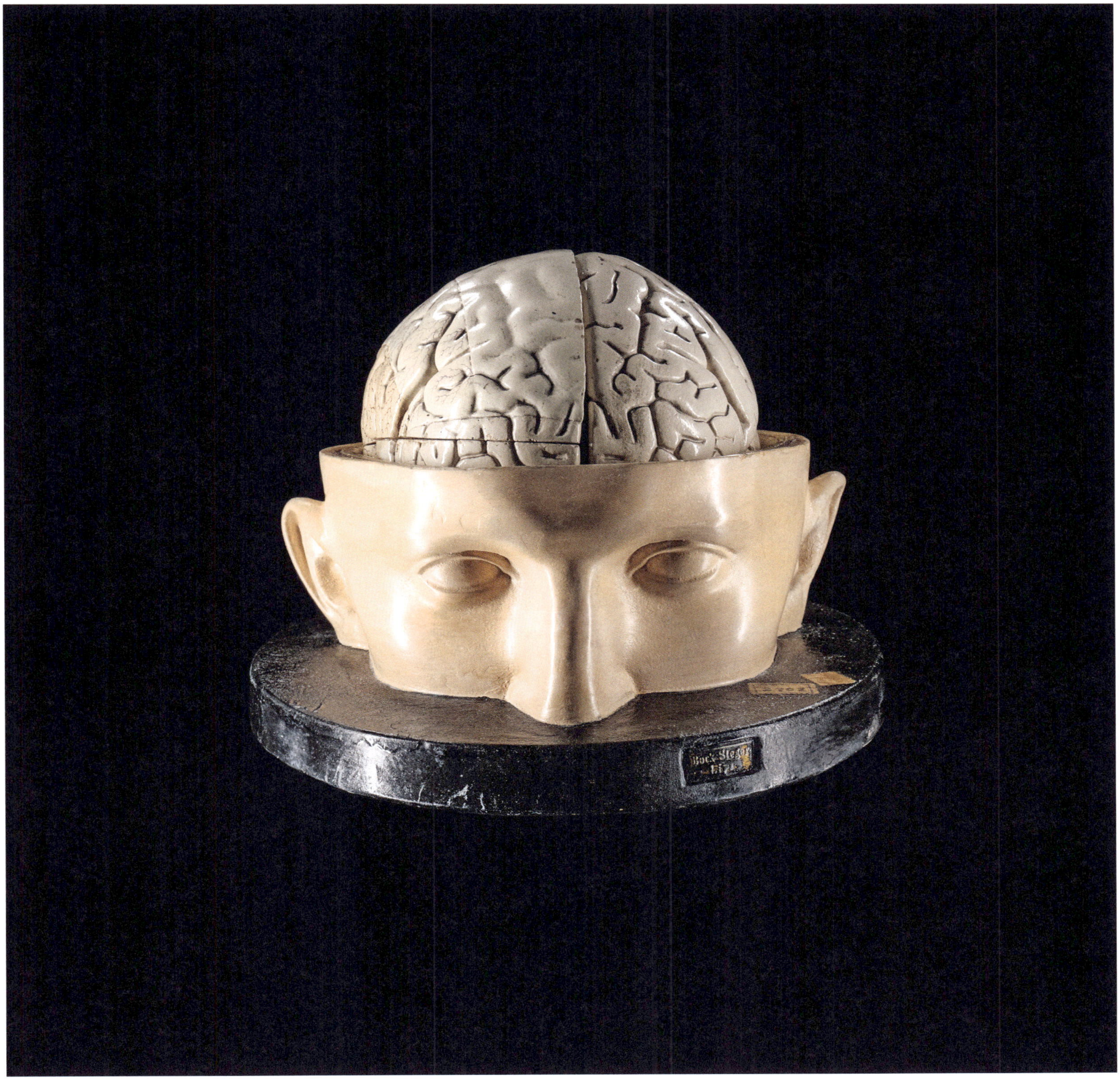

WHERE THE SOUL SINGS

"Art can sometimes be difficult to understand. But that is precisely what makes it so noble. It opens up a space for conversation and invites people to engage with it. When art and people come together, meaning is created."

Christoph Quarch

in which the creative spirit feels at home under a vast expanse of palm leaves, there will be small, secluded corners in future office districts where people can retreat to grow in secret and then emerge into the open with new fruits. Personal creativity and co-creativity are the two sides of the same process, from which strong personalities and mature individuals emerge: people who make a difference because they bring their potential to fruition through a lively exchange with others. Future office districts will take care to provide spaces for retreat, intimacy, and seclusion so that individuality and sociality complement each other in a fruitful way.

8. Prosperity—What is in bloom shows itself in all its splendor and beauty, has fully unfolded, and has come into its own. It is *prospering* (from the Latin *prosperare—to thrive*) and *flourishing* (from the Latin *flor*, the *flower*). Next, it will bear fruit and yield. This is the cycle of life. Beauty and yield, as well as aesthetics and functionality, are not mutually exclusive in the greenhouse. On the contrary, they are two aspects of value creation that follow not only the logic of production, but first and foremost the logic of cultivation. This combination of aesthetics and economy will be omnipresent in the office areas of the future: whether in architecture and furniture, interior design and color scheme—the aim will always be not just to satisfy the imperatives of efficiency and functionality, but to create an atmosphere that supports people in their growth and makes a good life possible. Future office areas will combine beauty and functionality, poetry and productivity, thereby ensuring that human development can keep pace with material or monetary growth. The usually sterile house of rational value creation will be transformed into a prosperous and flourishing garden of human potential development.

9. Entrepreneurship—The transformation of working environments along the lines of gardens and greenhouses will foster a new kind of entrepreneurship. Entrepreneurs of the future will resemble gardeners who cultivate people's workspace so that they can live well, and their skills can flourish to their fullest. Future entrepreneurs will no longer be producers, but curators: people who are committed to nurturing and caring for life, people who dedicate themselves to the *cura*—the *healing*—of the wounds inflicted on people's inner and outer lives by an economy that is far removed from nature; people who place themselves at the service of life; people who do not want to hand over the future of their company to the artificial intelligence of algorithms, but who take their responsibility for the vitality and humanity of life seriously. Such people will not shift their entrepreneurial responsibility onto machines but will see themselves as guardians and custodians of nature. Such people follow the appeal with which the philosopher Voltaire (1694–1778) ended his novel *Candide*: *Il faut cultiver notre jardin*. “We must cultivate our garden.”

EMBRYO

"From birth to death, every human being longs to repeat two experiences from the womb as often as possible.
1. Being connected to something greater than oneself.
2. Growing toward freedom—unleashing one's potential."
Gerald Hüther

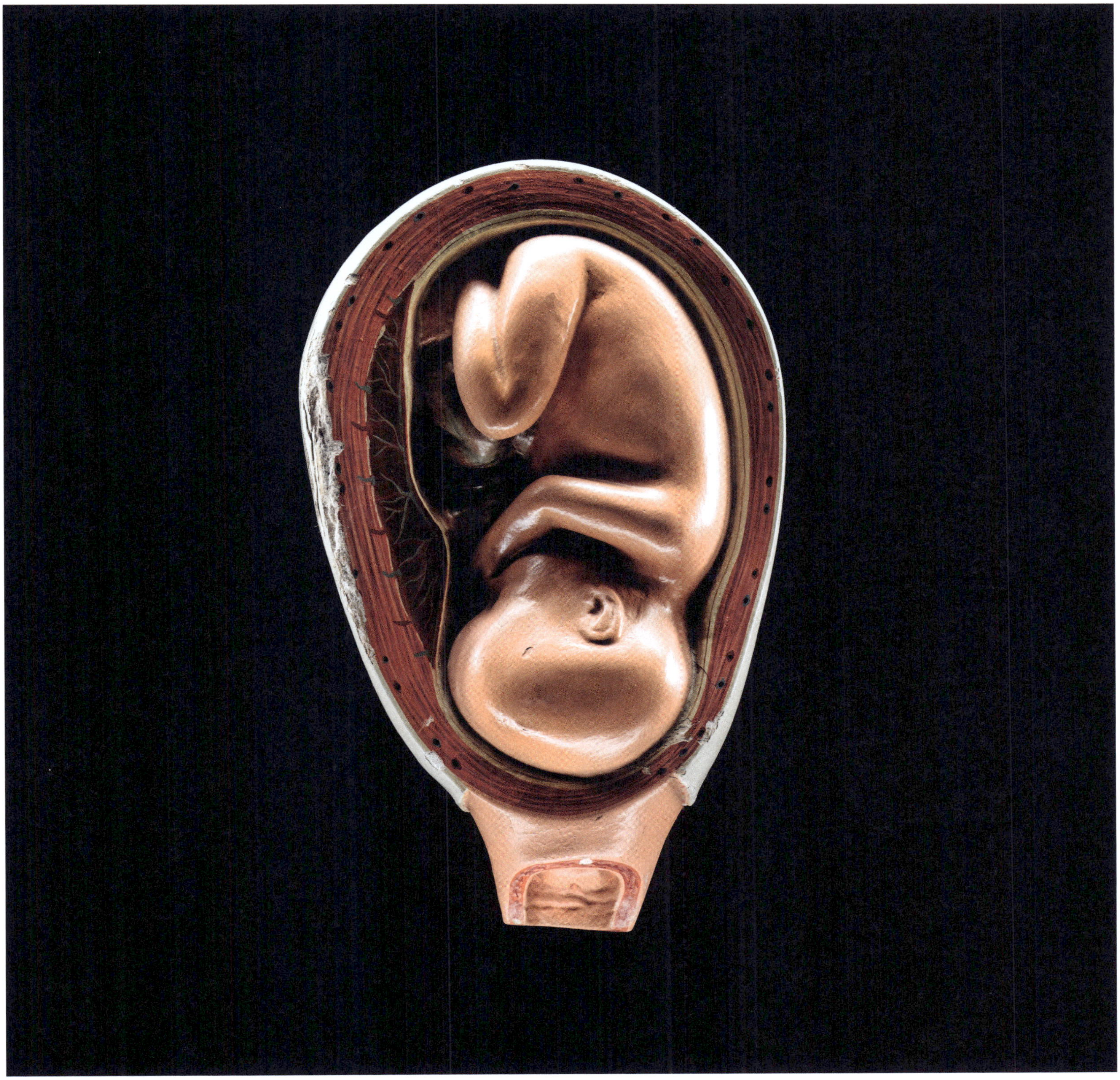

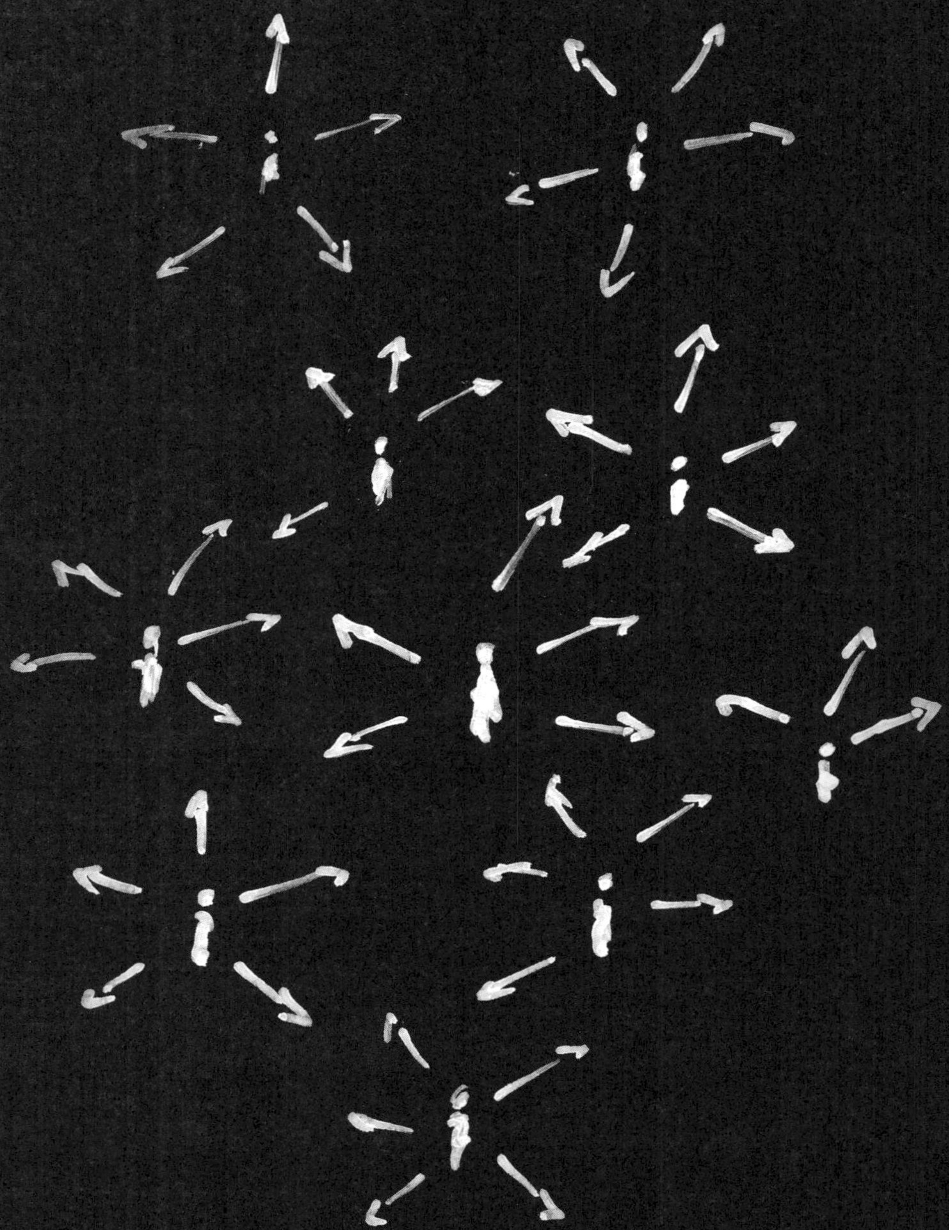

INTERVIEWS WITH
MICHELE DE LUCCHI
ROBERT THIEMANN
DORINE DE VOS
HANS ULRICH OBRIST
ANDREW TUCK
MICHAEL PHILLIPS
ROB SPEYER
LAURA HINES-PIERCE
FRANÇOIS TRAUSCH

WISDOM AND FORESIGHT

WISDOM AND FORESIGHT—If we speak with the architects, journalists, curators, designers, and real estate developers of today and at the same time look back at the heroes who inspired them, the question automatically arises: How did it ever get this far? With such wisdom and foresight, how could the coldness of turbo capitalism infiltrate the design of our workplaces almost unchecked? The following interviews demonstrate that it is never too late for a courageous transformation towards human-centered office environments, and we can be confident.

MICHELE DE LUCCHI

"WE MUST LEARN TO STUDY THE PRINCIPLES OF COOPERATIVE COMMUNITIES AND NOT THOSE OF BATTLES."

The interview with

MDL Michele de Lucchi was conducted by JT Jan Teunen.

JT Michele, you are a keen observer of the world. What do you consider the most important question facing us humans today?

MDL I don't want to avoid the big questions facing humanity, i.e., questions like: "Is there something we will never know?," "Do we believe in the unknown?," "Will we ever attain knowledge that can explain everything: the universe, time, past, and future?," "Will we ever know when existence begins and ends?," "What is beyond the universe?" But there is a new, more pressing question today.

It is: "Are the challenges we face getting out of hand?" In other words, "will we, as humanity, be able to take care of ourselves?"

JT Everyone desires, during their lifetime, to repeat two experiences granted to them in the womb: to be connected to something greater and to grow into freedom. How can architecture and interior design serve these longings?

MDL Architecture and design are not only technical but also, and above all, human fields. They try to understand the meaning people in different eras attach to their existence to apply the resulting beliefs and values to the contemporary world. To do this, they harness scientific discoveries and technological innovations. They also strive to solve significant problems, avoid major mistakes, and fulfill people's needs, desires, and expectations as much as possible. It is the task of designers and architects to propose behaviors for creatures like us—creatures who are aware of a higher purpose.

JT You believe in the concept of beauty. Why can beauty save the world, as Dostoyevsky once put it? [14]

MDL The concept of beauty encompasses, in a single word, everything we humans long for to improve our living conditions. Beauty is an essential element of the human spirit. I would not be surprised if, one day, we could prove that the symbolic language with which we, as the only living beings, were endowed was invented solely to express and transmit the wonder of beauty.

JT The COVID-19 pandemic forced many office workers to work from home. Now that the crisis is over, a high percentage of employees are refusing to return to the office. What do you think is the reason for this?

MDL I don't think it's a case of laziness or tiredness. People actually want an environment that stimulates them, in which they recognize themselves, and in which they feel part of a community. Only if they don't find all of this in their offices do they prefer to work from home. Offices that offer precisely that, on the other hand, are generally not given up. Apart from that, people are reluctant to travel long distances, partly due to the cost and partly due to the time involved in commuting. Above all, however, most offices lack appeal and charm. But it doesn't have to stay that way. Just think of restaurants in the immediate post-COVID period. They often had great appeal, and not just for eating. Going to a restaurant is about seeing people, meeting friends or interesting people, discussing, and catching up, without the stress and pressure of having to get anything done. It's simply about experiencing a different atmosphere and trying a wide variety of food. What I'm trying to say is that wherever possible, we should replace obligation with cooperation, passivity with self-efficacy, compulsion with personal interest. We should give people the opportunity to have new experiences, master new challenges, and fulfill exciting tasks that promote their personal growth.

JT Is this a recipe for bringing employees back to the company offices?

"THIS IS HUMANITY'S NEW AMBITIOUS PROJECT: NOT TO CONQUER THE WORLD, BUT TO CONQUER ITSELF."

MDL Yes, if offices can stimulate such changes, people will be happy to return there. Routines and ingrained habits are no longer accepted as success factors for working life. Above all, the new generations are looking for attractive, lively physical and social environments that are easy to change and can respond to new habits, interests, and even fashions. Health is a crucial issue that impacts everyone, regardless of age. The office is often where people spend the majority of their time, so it urgently needs upgrades and improvements compared to the comfort of their own homes.

JT According to the latest studies, 85 percent of the workforce is unmotivated. According to Buckminster Fuller, we should not try to change people, but the environment.[15] What qualities are needed in the office world to increase people's motivation?

MDL I personally believe in the power of inspiration and the positive influence of the environment on people's entrepreneurial spirit and creativity. Epigenetics has provided evidence of the interaction between people and their environment. This science examines the relationships between individual cells and their environment. The result is that cells obtain the information necessary for their development not only from the DNA, but above all from the membrane that surrounds them. This means that the information from the environment is much more important than the genetically transmitted data. This is because it has a major influence on the development of new cells. There are billions of cells in our body, and our behavior is the result of the interaction of all these cells. Consequently, the environment plays a crucial role in fostering motivation and inspiration. We have undervalued these insights for far too long.

JT What qualities must offices have today to foster human relationships? Or, to put it another way, how can architecture and interior design become a factor that nourishes and strengthens employees?

MDL The most important thing is to promote interaction: humanity has become strong through the spirit of cooperation. Hierarchies, on the other hand, have the opposite effect. It is much more important to encourage interaction than to give orders. In the era of artificial intelligence, this topic is becoming increasingly important for human relationships. This is because knowledge is now evenly distributed, and it is increasingly important to acquire both the ability to learn and the ability to unlearn. It has been proven that people react more quickly when they are in a positive mood. Against this backdrop, the role of design and architecture is to continually develop new, contemporary proposals for the design of spaces. If you want to be successful, you must constantly renew your offices and should therefore continually provide the most advanced environment for technology and human intelligence.

JT In his book *The Theater of Work*, Clive Wilkinson[16] claims that our world has turned into an over-engineered vehicle with too many ways to hit the brakes and a lot of sand in the gears. How can this problem be solved?

MDL Freedom and security are mutually exclusive. Those who are prepared to trade freedom for comfort and safety will certainly lose both. In recent decades, we have invested heavily in the security of facilities, environments, and work equipment. This was sensible and responsible. At the same time, however, it has also bloated bureaucracy and standardized numerous behaviors and processes. As a result, many people have settled into routines that they carry out automatically and with decreasing awareness. This happens at different levels. Therefore, we should initiate creative processes as much as possible to show everyone that there are no uncreative people and that we are all capable of tackling problems playfully and acting decisively. I really believe in this concept. If it catches on, creativity will be the most sought-after commodity of the future.

“I DO WHAT I WANT, I DO WHAT I LOVE, AND I DO WHAT I BELIEVE IN.”

JT Rabindranath Tagore wrote in his *English Writings* that, "the civilization of ancient Greece was nurtured within city walls. In fact, all the modern civilizations have their cradles of brick and mortar. These walls leave their mark deep in the minds of men. They set up a principle of 'divide and rule' in our mental outlook, which begets in us a habit of securing all our conquests by fortifying them and separating them from one another. We divide nation and nation, knowledge and knowledge, man and nature. It breeds in us a strong suspicion of whatever is beyond the barriers we have built, and everything has to fight hard for its entrance into our recognition."[17] Is it time to do without walls?

MDL I teach my students to build walls to unite and not to divide. Walls are necessary, but they should not become barriers of demarcation, physical or mental boundaries, or obstacles to cooperation. In my eyes, they are a means of living together. For designers, this requires a change in mentality: we must learn to study the principles of cooperative communities and not those of battles. There is an old saying that real mountaineers are not out to conquer a mountain, but themselves. This is humanity's new ambitious project: not to conquer the world, but to conquer itself.

JT For our *Lenbachgärten* project in Munich, we envision transforming the mechanical offices into a kind of greenhouse—transparent to the outside and connected to the original model of a house, in harmony with the cosmic order. What do you think of this vision?

MDL I once developed the concept of the "cultivation station." It is based on exactly this metaphor of a greenhouse, in which plants are cultivated, and seeds are protected. The "cultivation station" serves the development of ideas—a concern that must be pursued with the utmost care and conscientiousness. The real issue of the modern age, it seems to me, is fertility, not just because of the desertification of agricultural land or the decline in the number of children being born. Today, many young people are rightly fascinated by the issue of sustainability and concerned by the major social and climatic problems. With good reason, because we are in constant danger of destroying and devastating everything around us, including and above all the meaning of our lives. The idea of bringing people closer to the wonder of nature is undoubtedly the right one and can only be beneficial for both people and the natural world.

ROBERT THEMANN

ROBERT THIEMANN
Journalist and author,
founder of *Frame* magazine and Betterness

“IMPLEMENT THIS CHANGE FOR THE EMPLOYEES, BUT ABOVE ALL, WITH THEM.”

The interview with

RT Robert Thiemann was conducted by JT Jan Teunen.

JT Robert, the COVID-19 pandemic has led to a change in the world of work. Many employees have not returned to the office after experiencing the benefits of working from home. Companies are not always happy about this and want their employees to return to the office. How can they be persuaded to do so?

RT I know the story of a designer who, at the end of the pandemic, was asked to redesign a largely empty office so that employees would be happy to return there. Her meetings with the company's management were mostly held online. When she realized this, she declined the commission. Why, she asked herself, should the employees return to the office if the management didn't do it themselves? The moral of the story is the answer to your question: if you want to get your employees back to the office, managers need to lead by example.

JT In your view, is it desirable for work to move more from mobile work to the office again?

RT I firmly believe that the autonomy that employees have gained during the COVID period must be maintained. They have discovered that they can work just as productively and dedicatedly at home as in the office. Research has even shown that productivity has increased in many cases. Give your employees more responsibility and autonomy, and you will be rewarded with motivation and commitment, with some exceptions. And anyway, why should employees have to commute to their workplace in large numbers again? Not only do they lose valuable time, but they also lose their freedom. And in many cases, they are doing the environment a disservice.

JT In light of this, what would be your advice to employers?

RT Leave it up to the individual employees and self-organized teams to decide whether they want to come into the office or not. For some, it is important to have their colleagues around them, while others appreciate the peace and quiet and being alone. Don't make the mistake of lumping everyone together and demanding everyone's presence. Sooner or later, this will work against the company.

JT You recently founded BETTERNESS, an interior design consultancy. The working environment is one of the areas in which you are active. What is your most important piece of advice for redesigning the spaces we still call "offices"?

RT I can build on what I've just said: Don't just implement this change *for* the employees, but above all, *with* them. All too often, management commissions a design agency, which then submits a well-briefed proposal. However, this often overlooks asking employees about their needs. It is a top-down procedure. The result is, at best, a nice facility that manifests management thinking. And this often happens at the expense of the employees.

JT How can this danger be countered?

RT By ensuring that employees feel heard and seen. To do this, it is advisable to involve them in the design process: before, during, and after completion. This will make them feel like co-owners of their new workplace and give them more responsibility for it. Their sense of belonging will increase. They are also likely to use their workplace more often. Of course, there is a risk of creating a nondescript mishmash: something boring that nobody takes offense to, but that nobody likes either. This can be avoided by giving the designers the role of initiator and curator. They can then make suggestions, shape the ideas of the employees, and ultimately translate them into concrete decisions.

JT When it comes to the office, should

companies see themselves more as hosts than employers?

RT Absolutely. For a long time, employees were seen as machines that performed work. This work often consisted of monotonous administrative tasks: Making phone calls, correspondence, writing notes and summaries, or preparing reports. Then there were meetings, and all of this had to be managed from above. The offices provided a kind of shelter for the human machines and their managers.

Until, in recent years, they realized *en masse* and by necessity that much of their work could just as easily be done at home. As a result, the role of the office is changing. It will no longer house production workers, but employees who come to the office as guests for the day. And employers will become hosts.

JT But this is a role that they first have to learn.

RT That's true, but it's not difficult. You can learn a lot from the hospitality industry in this respect. Hosts usually welcome their guests in comfortable surroundings that stimulate their senses. The guest should want for nothing. In upmarket restaurants, this even goes so far as to push back the chairs and place the napkins neatly when going to the toilet. In hotel rooms, the curtains are drawn at night, a light is switched on, a glass of water is provided, a sweet is placed on the bedside table, and slippers are placed next to the bed. All this attention makes the guest feel welcome and appreciated. It doesn't have to be quite so extreme in the world of work, but there is an important question to take away from this: How can companies show that they really care about their employees?

JT Good working environments feel human. They address the four dimensions of the human being: the body, the soul, the spirit, and the self. Why does this happen so rarely?

“WORKPLACES WILL INCREASINGLY HAVE THE TASK OF CONNECTING PEOPLE WITH EACH OTHER.”

RT For decades, offices were not designed with people or employees at the center. Organizations created places for working people, but mainly for the glory of the organization, i.e., the employer. The focus was on production. At most, the culture of the employer should also be recognizable. But because the focus was on production, control was necessary. That was exercised by managers, who were therefore given the most beautiful rooms to ensure that the machine ran smoothly. I am overdrawing the picture to show how little room there was for the human element in this mindset. Real attention to and connection with the individual has only been around for a few years. Now, every person is different: everyone perceives stimuli differently, has unique needs, and simply doesn't function in the same way as another. It's not easy to create an environment where everyone feels seen and heard in all their facets—physical, mental, and even spiritual. This means that a work environment should offer as much diversity as there are individuals. And that is impossible. But more diversity seems to me to be the royal road to a more human environment.

JT What are you thinking about?

RT Rest and action, sitting still and movement, reflection and routine work, having a higher goal in mind and running in the background, zooming out and hyperfocus: all of this should be possible more or less everywhere at the same time, at the same workplace.

JT Why is there such a great need for green in the working world?

RT The pandemic has made it clear that health cannot be taken for granted. Many people have died, almost everyone has experienced the effects of the coronavirus first-hand, and governments have issued hygiene guidelines to prevent infection. While in the years before the pandemic, the importance of a healthy mind in a healthy body was recognized in small circles at best, health has now become a ubiquitous topic. Although this focus has since faded somewhat, the importance of well-being has remained. And that's where green comes in. Research indicates that people feel good when they are directly or indirectly connected to nature. This is why biophilic design has become so fashionable. It involves intensive contact with nature, for example with plants and trees, but also with daylight, clean water, and fresh air. Natural materials and shapes, even images from nature, also have a positive effect on human well-being. Advanced entrepreneurs know this. They also take advantage of the fact that a biophilic environment increases concentration. This should increase productivity and reduce absenteeism.

JT The arrival of artificial intelligence in offices means that routine work will slowly disappear. This will not be without consequences for offices. What will change?

RT Workplaces will increasingly have the task of connecting people with each other and accommodating groups. They will be much more social places than they are today.

Individual desks and the familiar meeting room with table, chairs, and screen will not disappear entirely from the offices of the future. But they will primarily be designed for brainstorming sessions, workshops, project meetings, training courses, and customer receptions. This will require a variety of spaces that can be easily adapted to a wide range of activities and group sizes. Some places will therefore have an unclear or vague use so that they can be quickly and easily adapted to different needs. In addition, new typologies will emerge where, for example, concentrated work can alternate with teamwork in the same space. This is an exciting challenge for designers.

JT How can designers solve this task? Or to put it another way: how can we create spaces that offer people a home that lasts beyond the day?

RT From my 26 years of experience as editor-in-chief of *Frame*, a platform for interior design, my editorial team and I have drawn up five principles to ensure that spaces have lasting meaning for their users and have as little impact on the planet as possible. These principles also apply to offices.

JT Would you like to share it with us?

RT Of course. The most important principle is to focus on the health and well-being of our employees. We have already discussed this at length. The second principle is an extension of that principle: don't dictate everything and let the employees help to shape it. Once again, you can only design for people if you design with them. Therefore, as a client and architect, give people a sense of responsibility, co-ownership, and belonging. This makes it easier to maintain a space well and to develop people. Focus both on the individuals and the connections between people. The third principle is to create space for experiences that have meaning for people.

JT What does that mean in concrete terms?

RT Specifically, it means that it's not about entertainment. Don't put an empty mini-golf course or some infantile swings in the office. Much better are quiet places, a crazy restaurant, a beautiful park, or a luxury movie theater. Exceed people's expectations by opening spaces for them to experience and benefit from.

JT Then we move on to the fourth principle ...

RT Exactly. The fourth principle states that spaces do not belong to anyone forever, not even to companies. We are all passers-by who use houses, stores, and offices for a certain period of time. After that, these spaces are passed on to others who will probably use them in an entirely different way. That is why spaces should be planned and built in such a way that they can be adapted to other wishes and needs without having to demolish them—in other words, without being wasteful with resources. In the best case, interiors are designed for the circular economy. The last principle is an extension of that principle: we must learn to minimize our impact on the earth. Anyone who builds uses materials and energy and therefore emits CO_2. We should limit this as much as possible by constructing fewer new buildings and reusing more existing buildings. We can also use more biomaterials and learn to build in an energy-neutral way. I believe we can continue with these five building principles for decades to come.

DORINE DE VOS

“OFFICES AND THEIR DISTRICTS URGENTLY NEED TO BECOME MORE ATTRACTIVE SO THAT PEOPLE WANT TO WORK THERE AGAIN.”

The interview with

DDV Dorine de Vos was conducted by JT Jan Teunen.

JT Dorine, in the early 1990s, you and your business partners, Hans Loos and Daan van der Have, transformed an office building in Rotterdam that had been vacant for 20 years into the highly acclaimed *Hotel New York*. Subsequently, the Kop van Zuid district was built around it, which is now considered a model for successful urban development. Tell us about this project.

DDV The project was under a lucky star right from the start. We were simply lucky. It started at the right time with the right people who had good plans for a good place. Riek Bakker, who became the new Director of Urban Development in 1986, was a visionary. She was not from Rotterdam and lived in a hotel on the banks of the Maas. From there, she looked out over a large, abandoned, poorly developed harbor area—120 hectares in size, with a few empty buildings and very poor connections to the city center. There were areas like this in all major port cities, including New York. The old harbor with its free port was banished from the city and relocated near the sea. Riek Bakker now considered how this abandoned area could be connected to the city center—how it could be transformed into an attractive residential and working district. The solution was a bridge that connected both sides of the river and thus the Kop van Zuid with the city of Rotterdam. At the same time, we developed our plans for the new purpose of the vacant headquarters of the *Holland America Line*. Even though the *Hotel New York* was initially a no-man's land, it immediately became a magnet. The new bridge made it easily accessible, and my partners began connecting the two banks with additional water taxis. Other buildings now surround the hotel. Many renowned architects have built there, including Rem Koolhaas, who designed the largest building in the Netherlands, as well as Renzo Piano and Bolles+Wilson, to name just a few.

JT What is the secret of the Kop van Zuid district?

“CO-CREATION WORKS BETTER IN THE OFFICE THAN AT HOME BECAUSE YOU MEET COLLEAGUES THERE AND CAN DISCUSS IDEAS, PROJECTS, AND PROBLEMS FACE-TO-FACE RATHER THAN VIA AN INTERFACE.”

DDV The special thing about it is that apartments, restaurants, theaters, museums, gastronomy, and offices are all together in a tiny space. However, there is also some criticism of the result: the whole thing is not human enough, it could be much more attractive with small stores and beautiful shop windows, with more greenery and less wind.

JT It all started with the transformation of the vacant office building. What is the state of the offices in the district today?

DDV Unfortunately, there has been a lot of vacancy here again since the pandemic. The digital revolution has made it possible to work flexibly from home. It is now impossible to imagine the world of work without it. As a result, many workstations in offices remain empty. Yes, entire floors are deserted, which I honestly can't understand at all. I'm constantly distracted at home. I would be surprised if others didn't feel the same. However, if I'm in a place where I can concentrate on my work—in my case, that's my studio—then I'm immediately in a working mood. Simply because there's little else I can do there, and I'm not distracted.

JT What role does meeting other people play in this?

DDV A big role. Co-creation works better in the office than at home because you meet colleagues there and can discuss ideas, projects, and problems *face-to-face* rather than via an *interface*. Of course, I know that many offices and neighborhoods are boring as hell. In Amsterdam, for example, there is the *Zuidas* neighborhood next to the city highway, where you can do field research on what happens when a district is the result of purely functional planning: monotonous buildings, mediocre cafés with mediocre food, office workers in bad suits. The whole thing may be efficient and suitable for financial brokers, lawyers, and the like, but it is by no means human. Many employees understandably relocate to the other side of the highway to work in the *Coffee Company* branches. Because there is a more attractive, lively, and poetic quarter there. This makes me wonder why my own company can't create such environments for its employees—neighborhoods where they can enjoy healthy, good food, celebrate rituals like writing with a fountain pen in a nice notebook, and more. It would not only be good for the brain, but also for identity, belonging, connectedness, and therefore motivation. People have always wanted to be seen and appreciated. It can't be attractive to be reduced to the size of a postage stamp on the screen while you're working from home.

JT But they still like to work from home.

DDV In the past, workers were dependent on their companies and their work. They felt responsible for the tasks they took on. That no longer seems to be the case today. That's why there are calls for a three or four-day week, with a simultaneous increase in pay. This cannot work. The world of work must change. Work is part of life, and free time does not necessarily make you free. That's why I say that offices and their districts urgently need to become more attractive so that people are motivated to return to work there again.

JT Speaking of more attractive, that is what the city of Dordrecht also wanted when it asked you to transform a water tower and water treatment plant into a hotel and restaurant. You accepted the challenge. Today, the *Villa Augustus* has a magnetic attraction. Why is that?

DDV Mainly because of the two gardens. They are the heart and soul of our project. One of our partners has lived on a country estate for a long time and has experienced firsthand the beneficial effects of greenery and nature, as well as the changing seasons. This is exactly what we wanted our guests to experience. We took our inspiration from Italian villas, which often have a magnificent garden for the reception. Guests were received there, and they have a kitchen garden for entertaining.

JT You have brought nature into the hotel and restaurant. And what about art?

"EVER SINCE I WAS 14, I'VE SPENT MY LIFE TRYING TO STAY 14."

DDV Art too, of course: the visual arts, but also music and literature. It's all food for the soul. When I go somewhere, I want to see a lot and many others do too: the eye has to travel! Whether this will continue to be the case in the future remains to be seen. I've noticed that many young people have fewer and fewer eyes for the beauty around them. They constantly stare at the screens of their cell phones and miss out on a lot as a result.

JT Somewhere out in the world, do you have a favorite neighborhood?

DDV My favorite cities are Paris and New York. I feel at home there. I prefer to spend time in neighborhoods where museums, galleries, bookshops, offices, restaurants, and cafés gather. That's where the social and cultural function of a neighborhood is taken into account. All is right with the world for me there.

JT Fyodor Dostoyevsky once said that "beauty saves the world." Do you think he was right?

DDV Yes, I am convinced of that. Beauty saves and heals in many ways: reading, seeing, eating, hearing, and smelling. Perhaps without realizing it, the next generation also believes this. Young people are constantly looking at their cell phones, but they spend huge amounts of money on looking good and beautiful. That gives me hope.

Färbergraben

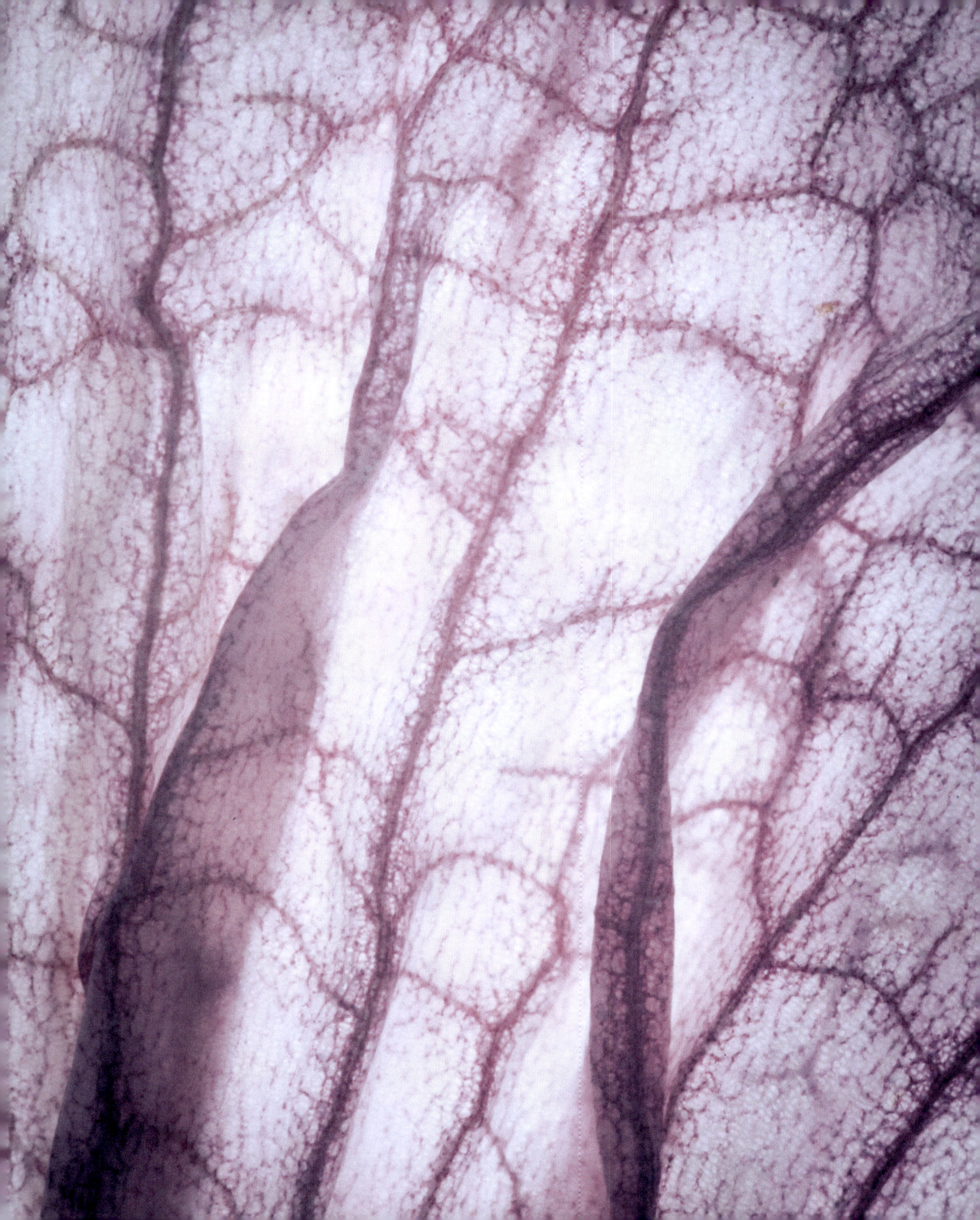

HANS ULRICH OBRIST

HANS ULRICH OBRIST
Author, curator, and artistic director
of London's Serpentine Galleries

"COMPANIES NEED ARTISTS."

The interview with

HUO Hans Ulrich Obrist was conducted by JT Jan Teunen.

JT Those who want to invent the future need to experiment. What experiments are you currently involved in?

HUO Experiments develop from conversations. Or even better: experiments are never-ending conversations. Let me give you an example: I have been the artistic director of the *Serpentine Galleries* in London for more than ten years. In the course of this work, it became clear to us that we needed to make structural changes to the organization of the museum. That's why we've set up three new departments: one for ecology, one for society, and one for innovative experiments in art and technology. To start with the latter: the Korean artist Nam June Paik proposed back in the 1960s to use new technologies to unleash international potential by matching art and technology. Billy Klüver followed a similar path with his E.A.T. *(Experiments in Art and Technology)* project, bringing together artists, scientists, and technology developers. Our experiment in London is proceeding in a similar way. In our department, we can develop video games with artists and through this, create new worlds. We experiment with AI and explore what artists can do with it—and how they can avoid potential dangers. The ethical handling of data also plays a role here—as does the question of what these new technologies mean for the entire ecosystem of arts.

JT Do the two other new departments you've set up also have this experimental character?

HUO Yes. Our ecology department is inspired by the German-English artist Gustav Metzger—a true pioneer of environmentalism—who in his work brought art and ecology together in ever new ways, steadily addressing the dangers of extinction. We've produced various campaigns and works of art in this tradition, some of which go beyond the scope of the museum. This brings me to the third department I mentioned: civic. Our aim here is to bring art into the world—especially to people who didn't grow up with art and don't go to museums. In this context, we've developed a project in which our artists, together with care workers, visit the Barking and Dagenham neighborhoods in London. So, in the three fields

“WHEN WE TALK ABOUT OFFICES, WE USUALLY THINK ABOUT SPACE, BUT I WONDER WHETHER WE SHOULDN’T ALSO THINK MORE IN TERMS OF TIME—GUIDED BY THE QUESTION OF HOW WE CAN MAKE BETTER USE OF OFFICE TIME.”

mentioned—technology, ecology, and society—I'm trying to shape the future through my work at *Serpentine.* But one thing remains clear to me: "The future flies in under the radar," as the artist Martha Rosler aptly put it.

JT You mentioned AI. Digital technologies are changing the world in which we live in many ways—including the world of work. After the pandemic, many employees have remained at home and continued working in virtual spaces. What needs to change to attract people to come back to the company office?

HUO When we talk about offices, we usually think about space, but I wonder whether we shouldn't also think more in terms of time—guided by the question of how we can make better use of office time. Many years ago, I had an employee who was always five to six hours late for work. He was brilliant, but this time behavior was hardly acceptable in an office environment. To solve this dilemma, I had a conversation with him, and it became clear that he was a real night person who simply couldn't work during the daytime. It was then that I realized that we live in a very homogenized world of time, in which each individual has to adapt to the prescribed office hours even if they don't correspond to one's working rhythm. As a result, I set up a separate night office for this employee, where he helps me with the preparation of my books as a "night producer."

JT Can you explain how that works?

HUO I stay in the gallery-office from 8 or 9 a.m. until 5 or 6 p.m., followed by a time slot for social commitments—lectures, openings, etc.—which I generally leave by 10 p.m. at the latest so that I can start the night shift and work with my night producer. Such a 24-hour office seems to me to be a very sustainable model, not only because it helps working people escape from the dictatorship of time, but above all from the perspective of ecological and economic efficiency. It's unfortunate that expensive constantly heated offices stand empty and unused at night and during the weekend.

JT Do you think there are enough people who'd like to work at night?

HUO Absolutely. I know this from my night producer—and from others who've recognized how productive the model is and therefore want to copy it.

JT Let's talk about the spatial aspect of the office. What needs to happen in the space to make people feel comfortable in offices again and to develop their potential?

HUO I'm neither an architect nor an office designer, and therefore not an expert on this subject, but I'd like to tell you one thing: at *Serpentine*, we have the former mayor of New York, the entrepreneur Mike Bloomberg as our chairman. Together with Architect Norman Foster, he's created a fantastic office building in London: *Bloomberg's* European headquarters. It's one of the most sustainable office buildings in the world—not only from an ecological, but also from a social point of view. There's an enormous amount of space in which employees can meet and interact. There's a food bar, where people can have co-creative conversations. Of course, it's not a new observation that in offices—just like at conferences—the most important things often happen during the coffee break—the unscripted, the unexpected—because this is where the linearity of everyday life is interrupted, and a situation is created in which people can deliver their thoughts. In addition to the ecological and social aspects, there's a third factor that makes the *Bloomberg* building so exemplary: the integration of art. Thanks to the work of Michael Craig Martin, we know about the positive, even healing influence of art in hospitals. It's not much different in offices. Here, too, art can have a positive impact on people. In the case of the *Bloomberg* building, for example, there's a fountain in the entrance area by Cristina Iglesias. Such installations create an atmosphere

"NOTHING WILL REMAIN AS IT IS. WE WILL HAVE TO PIVOT. AND WHO CAN DO THAT BETTER THAN ARTISTS?"

in which people feel safe. It seems important to me that the working environment in particular remains free of fear, but without giving people the feeling that they're working in a fortress.

JT This brings us to the topic of contextualization. Do you think that office buildings should communicate to employees what kind of company they work for?

HUO Absolutely. A building should make people understand where they are. In my opinion, anyone designing an office today should read the work of the Martinican philosopher Édouard Glissant.[18] Decades ago, he warned that in the age of globalization, we're in danger of homogenizing everything, and he argued that something needs to be done to counter this. At the same time, Glissant predicted that there would be a backlash: an attitude of anti-globalization that would lead to new regionalism and nationalism on the one hand and erode our tolerance and awareness of the fact that humans only really grow by conversing with others on the other. What office designers can learn from Glissant is that we should neither succumb to the temptation of homogenization nor to the danger of complete localization. It's important that offices don't look the same everywhere; they should respond appropriately to the local context.

JT Can you give an example to illustrate this?

HUO If I may return to the *Bloomberg* building, it's also an exemplary solution to this issue. The entire local history of the building's surroundings is taken into account here, starting with the Roman foundations that were excavated and made visible. This means that visitors and employees know what they're actually sitting on: not in a corporate building with no history, but in a place steeped in history.

This leads to another topic important to me with regard to sustainable offices: that parts of them need to be open to the public. In the *Bloomberg* building, there are arcades accessible to everyone, with restaurants, meeting facilities, and exhibition spaces. Through this, the building is connected to the neighborhood and serves a certain purpose for it. It welcomes the people who live there. This permeability seems very important to me—especially if you want to prevent the building from becoming an isolated fortress.

JT One of the wonderful projects you've worked on as a curator is the Art and Culture Complex of Maja Hoffmann's LUMA Foundation in Arles. What can future office environments learn from an area like this?

HUO Maja Hoffmann's vision was to create an institution that functions like a campus. The guiding idea was not to construct a homogeneous or standardized building, but to create what Édouard Glissant calls an "archipelago." He says: "In the archipelago, I can change through exchange with others without losing my sense of self." In the archipelago, according to Glissant, the merging—he speaks of "creolization"—of different cultures is possible without these cultures having to give up their identity. In my view, this is also important for office design: giving people the chance to change and develop through interaction with others. If you follow Glissant, this also requires something like flexible visions: not fixed utopias like Thomas More's, but something he calls "trembling thinking:" thoughts that remain agile and flexible. These considerations by Glissant are in the background of LUMA and have inspired the experimental character of the campus. This also includes the Atelier LUMA, where artistic production is carried out under ecological aspects.

JT What happens there?

HUO In the studio, designers, architects, and artists work with sustainable local materials, such as seaweed or natural products from the Camargue, to make them usable for today's design. Office designers can learn a thing or two from this: using local materials and making them visible. Another point is the archive, which plays an important role at LUMA.

“FOR REASONS OF INTERGENERATIONAL JUSTICE, WE MUST LOOK SEVERAL GENERATIONS INTO THE FUTURE, AND THEREFORE WE MUST MAKE OUR PROJECTS LONGER-TERM THAN THE DURATION OF A HUMAN LIFE, FOLLOWING THE EXAMPLE OFGAUDÍ’S CATHEDRAL, WHICH IS STILL UNFINISHED.”

It's not only about the history of the institution, but also about the stories of artists and other people. Behind this is the desire for visitors to engage with people's stories. These considerations can easily be transferred to office environments. It seems very important to me that companies are aware of their origins and history—especially as there are often very interesting company archives that could be made accessible to employees in office buildings. Studio and archive, production, and preservation: both seem equally important to me for the creation of office environments.

JT In addition to the studios, exhibition spaces and the archive, LUMA also offers residences for artists.

HUO It's good that you mention this. For me, it's always fascinating to see how the artists who live there for three months change not only the LUMA campus, but the entire city of Arles. Another project from the 1960s comes to my mind: the APG—Artist Placement Group—by British artists Barbara Steveni and John Latham, who proposed that every company, every organization, every public institution should employ at least one artist in residence. In the 60s, that was utopian. Today, it's a necessity. Just think of the climate emergency: a large part of our companies will have to change fundamentally. Nothing will remain as it is. We will have to pivot. And who can do that better than artists? That's why I recommend that when you design a new office building, don't forget a studio for an artist—a space where you can observe how new things will be created. And at the same time, give the artists a seat at the table where the decisions are made. The time has come for this: if we want to tackle the major challenges of the 21st century, then we should harness the expertise of artists.

JT In our book, we suggest using the greenhouse or garden as a new guiding metaphor for office environments: places that harmoniously combine economy and aesthetics. Do you like this idea?

HUO Very much. I can only endorse that. The metaphor fits very well at a time when we have to get beyond the short-termism of deadlines everywhere. Offices are often deadline machines, but in times of climate catastrophe, we must learn to think in long terms and work with broad time horizons. Today's office environments must incorporate this long duration and make us understand that we're only on this planet for a limited time span—but that we bear full responsibility for future generations; not only each individual employee, but also the company as a whole. This also applies to the art world. There are art fairs, galleries, museums; all of these are organized along the lines of events: vernissages, finissages, conferences, exhibitions, symposia. When I visit studios, however, I notice more and more often that artists are interested in long-term projects. For instance, we invited Alexandra Daisy Ginsberg last year. What do you think she had in mind? She really wanted to build a garden—a garden that wasn't just for people, but also for pollinators: bees and other insects. We got involved. The result was a pollinator garden designed with the help of AI, which was also aesthetically very interesting for visitors. We can also learn something from this for our office buildings: that they shouldn't be designed in anthropocentric ways only, but also give space to our fellow creatures. We should no longer use office plants lovelessly as decoration or room dividers but see them as friends and colleagues. We should hug trees and embrace plants.

321 3210

ANDREW TUCK

ANDREW TUCK
Co-founder and editor
of the global magazine *Monocle*

“AI WILL NOT COME AND DECORATE YOUR HOUSE, IT WON’T MAKE YOU A SHIRT OR PUT UP YOUR SHELVES.”

The interview with

AT Andrew Tuck was conducted by CQ Christoph Quarch.

CQ Andrew, *Monocle* is publishing books with titles such as *The Book of Gentle Living* or *The Guide to Better Living.* To which questions do these publications give the answers? Or in other words: Why do readers need and buy these books?

AT When we started the *Monocle* magazine in 2007, one of the central ideas was to focus on how you improve quality of life—and for everyone. How do you design cities where people have easy access to a great public realm, how do you create companies where staff feel valued, and how do you design schools to deliver better educational outcomes? *The Monocle Guide to Better Living* was our first book and it worked as a sort of modest manifesto, setting out how we saw the world, the nudges you could make to improve it too. *Gentle Living* came in 2020 and at a time when people were experiencing the pandemic and heightened political debates, and it was a success because it talked about living simply, choosing rewarding paths through life, doing work that you care about, being generous, listening. I hope people buy these books because they trust us to be open-minded, search the world for best practice, and find inspiring people doing amazing things.

CQ Humans spend lots of time at work. But work is changing rapidly. Soon AI will take over many routine operations. Which kind of work will still be carried out by humans in the future?

AT AI will not come and decorate your house, it won't make you a shirt or put up your shelves. It won't outsmart the analysts, the thinkers, the mavericks. Or the baker, the butcher. We always have waves of panic when technological advances take place but, in the end, they get woven into our lives in ways that soon become banal. And I also believe that journalism will survive—AI is good at repeating what's already known but that's not the job of a writer or editor.

“WHEN YOU ARE SURROUNDED BY YOUR COLLEAGUES, TAKING HUNDREDS OF SMALL BUT VITAL DECISIONS EVERY DAY, MAGIC HAPPENS.”

CQ During the pandemic, many companies pivoted to remote work as a necessity. It turned out that many tasks can be done effectively at home. Why does it still make sense for employees to stop working remotely on occasion and physically come into the company?

AT The world of work has shifted in extraordinary ways since the pandemic and all businesses have had to devise a model that suits their ambitions and needs. At *Monocle* we decided to come back to the office, fully, as soon as the rules allowed and I am so pleased we did. Making magazines, producing radio shows, publishing books are all intense, fast-paced, collaborative enterprises. During the lockdowns we managed to make all these things happen but everything was slower, a little ponderous, often lacking those sudden genius moments of team inspiration. When you are surrounded by your colleagues, taking hundreds of small but vital decisions every day, magic happens. I also think it's socially important—being able to interact with people, share stories, laugh together is vital. I realize some people have jobs where they are less valued or more a cog in a machine. But the office, done well, can be an amazing place.

CQ What aspirations and needs of employees need to be addressed by today's working places?

AT The strange thing is that in many businesses it's the older staff with pleasant houses and established families who are most reluctant to come to the office. Yet their absence denies many young staff the very thing that made them successes—a mentor. So, the workplace should be somewhere that's inspiring, that welcomes you into a company culture, that helps shape your future working life. And offices should be social—they should be designed in a way that brings people together, provides modern equivalents of the "water-cooler moment" where you get to have coffee, talk about ideas that are tangential to your core work. The office does not need to be reinvented as a children's playground with slides and beanbag seats, but it should be a space that people want to work in.

CQ What can architects and designers do to make employees feel comfortable at their offices?

AT In numerous businesses people work from laptops, need to have dozens of ad hoc and fast meetings, move from collaborative to focused work several times across a day, so you are seeing office and office-furniture designers embrace this. They are creating spaces where a call can be taken in silence, sofa areas where people can meet with another colleague or just perch with that laptop. I recently visited the London headquarter of the global property company *Hines* and they have pulled this off with perfection. Offices and domestic design have both learned lessons from each other.

CQ Will art and interior design play a greater role in planning office spaces in the future?

AT I think they always have. And here you have to be a little careful because not all interior design is good. Too often some bright paint and colorful sofas are offered as the solution for creating a fun work environment. But design is a discipline, and you should start with the basics—how do people want to use this space, what will make them feel focused and at ease. When you have worked out all those human elements, then you can start thinking about the soft furnishings. Art—it can be empowering but in many corporate offices it's parked there like a sports car, more status symbol than tool for staff inspiration.

CQ One of next year's megatrends will be a desire to live closer to nature and to achieve sustainability. How will this affect future office spaces?

“THE OFFICE DOES NOT NEED TO BE REINVENTED AS A CHILDREN’S PLAYGROUND WITH SLIDES AND BEANBAG SEATS, BUT IT SHOULD BE A SPACE THAT PEOPLE WANT TO WORK IN.”

AT Not just because of the pandemic, but access to outdoor space, fresh air, is desirable. In Paris, the 44-storey *Tour St-Gobain* designed by *Valode and Pistre* architects shows how this can be achieved even in a skyscraper—all staff have access to outdoor space, it even has a sky garden. We are also seeing many businesses relocating to city cores again—why be a life-sciences company in a rural headquarter when you could take office space in a cool neighborhood where you have a better chance of attracting young employees?

HIRMER

MICHAEL PHILLIPS

"FUTURE NEIGHBORHOODS WILL RESEMBLE VILLAGES."

The interview with

MP Michael Phillips was conducted by CQ Christoph Quarch.

CQ Michael, we all know that we can't predict the future, but we can certainly help shape it. You do this with the projects you realize. What are your most exciting construction projects at the moment?

MP Oh, there's quite a lot. Mostly it's about revitalizing old industrial areas. A good example of this is *Raleigh Iron Works* in Raleigh, North Carolina. There, we are in the process of transforming an old ironworks into an innovative neighborhood with offices, restaurants, gyms, breweries and event venues. Or take the *Navy Yard Charleston* project, where a community-focused neighborhood is currently being created in which offices, flats and shops will be located on a historic naval base. In Europe, we are working on an *Innovation & Design Building* in Lisbon and the *Schinkel District* in Amsterdam. An extremely creative area has been created there on the site of a former bicycle factory, which not only houses a variety of local shops, cafés, galleries, and even a distillery, but also innovative companies from the solar, fashion, and music industries. I would also like to mention the *Groot Handelsgebouw* in Rotterdam—a huge complex that we are helping to remodel together with E.ON. And that's not all, because we are also currently realizing a whole series of projects with Google in the USA.

CQ That's not a small number. Is there something that unites this multitude of projects—an idea or vision that you are pursuing?

MP Yes, we want to create multi-use neighborhoods: neighborhoods that are attractive and appealing—that invite people to live, work and play there. To do this, they need an environment in which they feel nourished both at work and in their families and leisure time. This is the goal that all the projects mentioned are pursuing in equal measure. It is always about putting together a puzzle that uniquely connects everything that makes people feel good. This is the case with all the projects we are involved in.

CQ Could one also say that they are concerned with creating neighborhoods in which the gap between work and life is bridged in order to achieve a work-life balance?

MP I would rather talk about *work-life integration.* Our aim is to find out what needs to happen so that people can move seamlessly between all the aspects of their lives that are meaningful to them. Our aim is to offer the right options and reduce potential breakpoints.

CQ Do you see specific needs or desires of people that you want to address with the areas you have developed?

MP We are convinced that people feel most comfortable in imperfect environments. We pursue a concept that we call *low architecture*—not the *high architecture* of *starchitects* who want to have a direct influence on people. We're about creating a welcoming, modest and accessible environment that people feel is a natural extension of their lives; that they might experience as a continuation of their childhood or their time at university; not so much as something unattainable that they aspire to, but as something familiar that they associate with sensory impressions from their childhood or other phases of their lives. This is a different approach to what has been done in the last thirty years, when we tried to keep away from the masses and didn't ask ourselves what makes ordinary people tick, what they feel or what they long for. We take a different approach. We don't want to intimidate people, we try to think from the bottom up and not patronizingly from the top down. And that's not so easy. It's both an art and a science. But that's exactly our DNA; that's what we're all about.

CQ Speaking of art. What role do interior architecture, design and art play in your vision of future neighborhoods?

“WHETHER A PROPERTY IS BROUGHT TO LIFE DEPENDS ON WHETHER PEOPLE PARTICIPATE IN THE EVENTS THEMSELVES OR WHETHER THEY JUST LOOK AT IT FROM THE OUTSIDE.”

MP Art is essential—especially the dialogue or interplay of the arts, whether it's fine art, sculpture or gardening and landscaping, or the culinary arts in the restaurants. It's all about cultivating people's different talents and bringing them together. In other words, it's about developing a living ecosystem that incorporates visual arts and music as well as sound and light. This means providing people with creativity so that they can turn to it and engage with it. But it also means stimulating creativity in the very places where people spend their time: encouraging them to be creative in their offices and homes.

CQ What can this look like in concrete terms?

MP It starts with giving people ideas—showing them something that makes them see the world through different eyes. This is followed by questions: How far can I get involved here? What kind of access do I have to this world: be it to a tech-savvy, digital world or to the analog world of events, seminars and lectures? Whether a property is brought to life depends on whether people participate in the events themselves or whether they just look at it from the outside. Both are art: the designed physical environment of the property as well as the programmatic environment with which it is operated. The aim is to encourage people to experience themselves as co-creators of their environment and to have a say in what happens in their neighborhood—regardless of whether they work, walk or shop there.

CQ In this book, we propose designing future neighborhoods or areas along the lines of a garden or a greenhouse: as buildings whose primary aim is to generate vitality. You obviously share this vision.

MP Absolutely. And that leads me to tell you about a building that we haven't talked about yet: the *Innovation and Design Building* in Boston, in which our colleagues from E.ON are also involved. It's a complete ecosystem that I immediately thought of when you mentioned the garden. Everything in a garden is cross-fertilized. Not only do the bees pollinate the flowers, the plants also pollinate each other. Through this method, nature ensures that fertility and creativity never cease and that new life can always emerge. This is exactly what we focused on with the *Innovation and Design Building.* We have created an ecosystem there that has brought together a wide variety of players. The results are co-products from our tenants: The industrial design company *Continuum* develops a special piece of furniture there for another customer, which is then trialed as a prototype in the studio of another tenant—in this case a software company. It is then sold via the showroom of the *Boston Design Center,* which is also located in this building complex.

This example shows how successful cooperation between tenants can be realized in a property designed as an eco-system. Or another example: do you know the sporting goods manufacturer *Reebok?*

CQ Of course.

MP *Reebok* once produced a limited edition shoe that was designed by *Continuum* and then completely sold by the 3,000 tenants of the neighborhood via an app. Your greenhouse metaphor makes me think of this kind of cooperation: a regenerative collaboration that benefits everyone. And then something else comes to mind: for us, our neighborhoods are about enabling communities that can become firmly rooted there, thereby becoming regenerative and living on even when our support has come to an end. Our aim is not to keep a neighborhood for three or five years and then leave it to its own devices, but to look after it until it makes a lasting contribution to the positive development of its surroundings.

CQ Today, we are not only talking about regenerative neighborhoods, but also about a regenerative economy. Could the projects you have realized be exemplary for a future sustainable economy?

MP I think so, at least they are designed for sustainability to a high degree that you don't find elsewhere. Maybe it's not such a great analogy, but I'm thinking of the issue of climate

"BECAUSE THAT IS EXACTLY WHAT CHARACTERIZES A GREAT PLACE: IT ALLOWS ALL PEOPLE TO COME TOGETHER AS A COMMUNITY IN THEIR INDIVIDUAL IDIOSYNCRASIES, WAYS OF WORKING OR VALUE SYSTEMS."

change. Because—to stick with the garden metaphor—we know one thing: the more firmly rooted a plant is, the more resilient it is to wind and weather, drought and aridity. And a resilient economy is exactly what we will need in the future.

CQ And if we apply this to the architecture of the future?

MP Great places with great architecture—whether it's *high* or *low architecture*—will be long-lasting and sustainable if they manage to connect with the souls of the people who live and work there; if they allow these people to put down roots in them. This is actually about the ethos of your German culture: to create something lasting, to do it well, to pursue good intentions. This is also part of our corporate culture, which has its roots in Germany by no coincidence.

CQ Now, longevity, sustainability and durability are not necessarily the values pursued by a global economy that is primarily geared towards short-term profit. Are the neighborhoods you have developed a kind of counter-world to this? Laboratories for the future society; or glass houses in which a better future is experimentally anticipated.

MP Our company is firmly rooted in values that are now associated with the formula ESG: *Environmental, Social and Governance.* We want to construct regenerative buildings that provide space for regenerative communities—and therefore generate a good return for their investors. This is only possible with investments and long-term thinking. A short-term investment strategy is incompatible with our business field. We are interested in long-term results, which are often only achieved after two or three rental periods, but are then very stable.

CQ How are the tenants who live and work in the areas you have created doing? What kind of feedback do you get?

MP We receive a wide range of feedback from our tenants. The majority is very positive. This is reflected in the fact that we have a long tenant retention rate and low fluctuation. This results in high tenant productivity. They generally tell us that they are satisfied. The only thing that bothers them is construction work.

CQ Is there anything that your tenants particularly want?

MP I keep hearing that tenants want local companies and shops as neighbors. Large outlets or branches of nationally operating companies are not so popular.

CQ From a European perspective, it sounds as if your tenants want to live in a kind of village where they can find everything they need to live and work in a small space.

MP We sometimes casually say that we strive to build a kind of spiritual high street that makes people feel at home: the place where they find their partners when they are young, where they celebrate their children's birthdays, where they celebrate their football team's victories, where they buy presents for their teachers and celebrate together. If we do our job well, this sense of belonging is created—without people even realizing it. I think we humans are very much characterized by routines. We always go to the same restaurants and always order the same dishes. Our aim is to create places that promote such routines and thereby convey a strong sense of home, where they know: they go there and get what they expect; and sometimes they encounter something surprising that gives them new ideas. That's exactly what happens in a village. And that is exactly what a *mixed-use neighborhood* can do.

CQ We now live not only in the physical, analogue world, but increasingly also in a digital, virtual world. Can the neighborhoods you have created help people find a balance between physical and virtual reality?

MP Yes, and there's even more to it than that: it's about creating low-threshold spaces where people who are not yet digitally socialized can come together with *digital natives:* Spaces where everyone feels at home. We offer digital apps, simple login options, great network coverage: all things that create a perfect digital environment and allow *digital natives* to get involved in such a physical environment. But there is also the opportunity for *non-digital natives* to feel at home in these neighborhoods. I am thinking of the mystery of today's airports. I'm used to going to the counter, checking in, getting a printed boarding pass, and chatting to the staff. But now you just go to a machine—and you only talk to people if you fail at the machine; an interesting phenomenon where the human encounter only takes place when you are unsuccessful. But no matter. What matters to us is building bridges between people—and between people *and* machines. Because that is exactly what characterizes a great place: It allows all people to come together as a community in their individual idiosyncrasies, ways of working or value systems—completely regardless of their age differences, completely regardless of their technological, sexual, or ethnic diversity, completely regardless of their different tastes. And that implies that such a place must remain fundamentally modest. You can't offer high-end flats that are super exclusive and super restrictive if your aim is for people to come together in such a place.

"THE IMPORTANCE OF PLACE: HOW REAL ESTATE AND PEOPLE-CENTERED DESIGN ACHIEVE GOOD RETURNS."

ROB SPEYER

“WE USE ART AS A PLACE MAKING TOOL. OUR AIM IS TO MAKE PEOPLE FEEL SOMETHING.”

The interview with

RS Rob Speyer was conducted by CQ Christoph Quarch.

CQ Having read the *Tishman Speyer* webpage, I found a compelling quote: "At Tishman Speyer, *we are committed* to building *community."* Why do you hold that building community is of utmost importance in the 21st century?

RS People want to connect with each other. They need real networks, not just an online network. That's what attracts people to cities and to real neighborhoods. About ten years ago, I challenged our entire organization to shift their focus to cultivating community. I asked them to spend more time learning who our customers are. People have so many choices for where they spend their time. To attract them, buildings need to be special and social, inclusive and inspiring. So, we set out to make our buildings great places to work, live, eat, and drink. This was as important to our business as it was to the neighborhoods and cities our buildings are in. It became even more important after the COVID-19 pandemic. A lot has been written about how to get people out from behind their screens. All of our buildings are the kinds people want to be in. It's the community element that no computer screen can replicate.

CQ What can be done by one of the biggest real estate companies to meet this need for community and connection?

RS A lot! We can activate spaces through physical design and programming to make them distinctively engaging. In late 2022, we completed a new commercial building on Manhattan's Far West Side, *The Spiral.* It is a perfect example of how we can curate a sense of place and community. When you walk into the lobby, the first people you see are our greeters. They smile, say hello, they know your name. Sometimes they even dance to the music we play throughout all of our lobbies. True story: one of the greeters at *The Spiral* regularly dances in the lobby. People love it! We've heard from customers that seeing her is one of the best moments of their day. Next, you notice our signature scent, the greenery planted throughout the lobby, and the museum-quality art that hangs on the walls. The Spiral's lobby is an avenue block long and double-height, so art is key to making the space feel human-scale. Then, maybe you start your day by getting coffee on the 66th floor. That space is what we call the *Clubhouse.* We chose to make that highest floor—the most valuable real estate in the building—a communal space. So, anyone who works in the building can go there. It has lounge seating, a café, meeting rooms, and an outdoor terrace. And on that terrace is the highest planted tree in New York City. The views from the floor are amazing, and people react really well to the space. It not only stands out to everyone I've visited it with, it has very much helped us lease floors throughout the building. While all of these things are good for people, and good for building community, they are also good for business. We have seen that this is the kind of office experience people want now. In an environment where you really have to compete for customers' business, especially office customers, it's important to deliver exactly what they want and more.

CQ One of your main focuses is the creation of dynamic, "large-scale urban neighborhoods." Can you explain this vision by referring to one or two examples already realized by Tishman Speyer?

RS The first example that comes to mind is a neighborhood called *The Springs* in Shanghai. We developed a 10-million-square-foot mixed-use project that has residential, retail, office, hotel, and entertainment space, along with a beautiful environmental preserve. When you go there, it is bustling. People are meeting friends for coffee or a meal. People are outside taking a break from work. It is a complete neighborhood. Another example is in San Francisco. We are developing a neighborhood called *Mission Rock* in a joint venture with the *San Francisco Giants.* The Port of San Francisco previously used the land, mostly for parking. But it has spectacular views of the San Francisco Bay. When we're done, the neighborhood will have office, residential, retail, and lab space. We already have customers and residents in the neighborhood. A 5-acre park ties it together. The park is both an amenity and a resiliency measure. It is elevated above projected future sea levels to defend

“WE AIM TO DO THIS IN EVERY OFFICE BUILDING WE MANAGE—THE GOAL IS TO CREATE THE FEELING THAT YOU ARE ARRIVING SOMEWHERE SPECIAL, DYNAMIC, AND ENGAGING.”

against flooding. One key to making this a neighborhood was our design team. Instead of hiring one architect to do the masterplan and all of the buildings, we hired a team of architects to work together. Jeanne Gang led the group and also designed one of the residential buildings. She really set a vision for the neighborhood's design. But other firms had the leeway to design specific buildings, keying off of that vision. The overall effect is that there is a common vocabulary for the neighborhood, but not uniformity. It worked really well. So well that we've replicated the team model at another neighborhood-scale development we're doing with Harvard, the *Enterprise Research Campus.*

CQ Since the COVID-19 pandemic we globally observe the trend that employees stay away from offices in order to work at their home desks. Now, companies realize that through this the sense of belonging and connectedness erode. How can architecture and real estate development contribute to making offices more attractive again?

RS We've also heard this from our customers. Many of them want their employees back in the office more of the time. They know it would be better for their culture and their bottom line. We see ourselves as a partner to help them get there. Our approach has been to make the office a place people want to spend time. And to make sure they have what they want to do outside of work nearby—restaurants, shopping, entertainment. Within the office, it's all the things I mentioned at *The Spiral*. We aim to do this in every office building we manage—the goal is to create the feeling that you are arriving somewhere special, dynamic, and engaging. It makes a difference. Take *Rockefeller Center.* That's where our greeter program first took off. I hired a man named Correll Jones—he goes by C.J. I noticed him at a private club on Fifth Avenue. He was the doorman, and I saw that he wasn't just staying at the door. When there wasn't anyone coming or going, he would walk around the sidewalk and talk with everyone. He not only knew all the members, he knew the neighbors! That's what I wanted in our office buildings. So I brought him here. Now he's like the mayor of *Rockefeller Center.* He's usually in the center plaza, in uniform, talking to people who walk through. He makes everyone feel welcome.

CQ Currently, there's a lot of talk about human-centric or human-oriented working environments. How does this affect you?

RS This is very connected to what we've done throughout our buildings. Even though it's trendy now, we've been doing it for years. We launched our global amenity platform, ZO, in 2017. Through ZO we host events, offer wellness services, and partner with local retail and restaurants. We also built shared spaces called ZO Clubhouses. They resemble social clubs with coffee bars and living rooms. ZO gives our customers one central place to go for all the things they might want while they are at work, or after hours. Anyone who works in a *Tishman Speyer* building has access to ZO programs, spaces, and benefits anywhere in our portfolio.

Our coworking business, *Studio,* is another example. Through *Studio,* we give customers a sophisticated, turnkey option for office space. This includes private offices, open desks, conference rooms, event spaces, and all the services that go along with a *Tishman Speyer* office. These programs work well together. And they reinforce all the things we do in our properties. They build community in the workplace. Helping people meet each other when they don't work together or even work at the same company. Making people happier and more effective by offering more than just a desk.

CQ In our book we propose to substitute the current key metaphor of economy and corporations by another one and to envision offices as greenhouses and gardens instead of sterile machines. Does this mental paradigm-shift make sense to you?

“WE FOCUS ON CREATING PLACES THAT ENRICH PEOPLE’S LIVES, CONTRIBUTE TO THE VITALITY OF CITIES, AND STAND THE TEST OF TIME.”

RS In a very literal sense, yes. We have put a lot of effort into biophilic design. You can see this at *The Spiral*, with planted terraces on every floor. You can visit *Radio Park,* a fully landscaped park on the roof of *Radio City Music Hall,* that is open to everyone who works at *Rockefeller Center.* In a metaphorical sense, this reflects a shift in work culture. I think it is about offering spaces for people to work in different ways. We've applied this in our own offices. Globally, our offices now include open desks and spaces for meetings, gatherings, and quiet work.

CQ One of the prior desires of generations to come seems to be reconnecting with nature. Again, by referring to exemplary projects: How can nature be integrated into future working environments?

RS We accomplish this in projects like *The Spiral,* where terraces are an integral part of the building's design. Or at *Mission Rock,* where *China Basin Park* is a major feature of the project and the new neighborhood. And at the *Enterprise Research Campus,* where an open space is both a resiliency and a recreational feature. We aim to do this in all our projects, whether through interior or exterior greenery. Because it's clear that people want to be able to see and touch something natural during their day.

CQ Do you think that art is required to generate attractive workplaces?

RS Art is an integral part of *Tishman Speyer* projects. So, for us, yes. As a company, we've been doing this for nearly 40 years. It started when my father put the 25-meter *Hammering Man* by Jonathan Borofsky outside of *Messeturm* in Frankfurt. People embraced it.

It became a symbol of the city. We use art as a place making tool. Our aim is to make people feel something. To make a space come alive. To start a conversation. Art can reinforce corporate culture, but it's also very personal. People may love or not love a piece. The point is for them to feel something.

CQ May I ask you to close your eyes and envisage the office you would love to spend time in?

RS It's where I already spend my time—my standing desk on the open floor in our space at *Rockefeller Center.* I can easily interact with the people I work with. It's efficient and I prefer working there. We have lots of rooms with tables or tables and screens. I use one of these when I'm on a video conference or so that I can sit down and have a conversation with a colleague. There is art and greenery throughout the office. Any direction you walk, you can see a colorful piece of art and planted greenery. And the rest of *Rockefeller Center* is just downstairs. The restaurants and shops here have become really popular with New Yorkers. I take that as a sign that we're doing something right.

23

graben

LAURA HINES-PIERCE

“IT ALL STARTS WITH PEOPLE.”

The interview with

LHP Laura Hines-Pierce was conducted by CQ Christoph Quarch.

CQ Even before your appointment as Co-CEO at *Hines,* you were already preparing the company for the future in your role as Transformation Officer. In your opinion, what are the most important challenges currently facing the real estate industry?

LHP Looking to the future, I would say that ESG *(Environmental, Social, and Governance)* and innovation are the two most important trends. This includes utilizing groundbreaking technologies and data to drastically reduce our environmental impact. I am particularly concerned about the CO_2 emissions of our more than 1,500 properties. We are striving to achieve this by leveraging innovations in renewable energy and construction methods to reduce carbon dioxide emissions down to zero. As the pace of innovation in the real estate industry is now catching up with that of other industries, my primary focus has been—and continues to be—on positioning *Hines* at the forefront of this movement.

CQ Many companies are concerned with the question of how to establish a people-centered organizational culture. What does this concept mean to you?

LHP My guiding principle is that everything starts with people. Every person at *Hines* has the opportunity to make a decisive contribution to achieving our goals. In doing so, we do a lot of good for our communities, the development of our cities, and our employees. We are seeking individuals who strive to excel and seize opportunities to be entrepreneurial in their own unique way. Our employees are always expected to do the right thing—because that is what ultimately keeps us alive as a company.

CQ You were part of the founding team of the *OneHines Women's Network,* which played a key role in aligning the company with diversity and inclusion. Why are diversity and inclusion so crucial for the economic success of future companies?

LHP There are many reasons for this ... but one of my most important professional goals is to close the gender gap in the real estate industry. As a woman in the executive suite of one of the world's largest real estate companies, I am fortunate to have a platform that allows me to make a difference in this area. At *Hines,* we continually strive to promote our female executives and hire more women. We know from experience that this is the right thing to do, because we see every day that diversity at all levels of our company helps us achieve better results for our clients.

It is fair to say that our *OneHines* initiative plays a key role in building an inclusive culture where all *Hines* employees feel valued and have equal opportunities to reach their full potential. Just imagine: today, 40 percent of our 4,850 professionals are women. This indicates that we are making genuine progress in developing a workforce that accurately reflects the society we live in. But we are also aware that we still have a lot more to do. I am personally committed to achieving this goal both within *Hines* and across the industry as a whole.

CQ What influence can a company like *Hines* have on making people feel comfortable in the office?

LHP Following the COVID-19 pandemic, it was urgently necessary to conduct detailed analyses of what office spaces need to offer to provide real added value to companies. At *Hines,* we believe that an office should be a "magnet, not a mandate." We are convinced that companies should view their real estate as a means of attracting talent. On the other hand, they should also see it as a tool that helps the company achieve optimal performance—just as good and innovative technology can do. That's why we often work side by side with technology. Our customers often tell us that one of their biggest challenges is attracting and

“AT HINES, WE BELIEVE THAT AN OFFICE SHOULD BE A ‘MAGNET, NOT A MANDATE.’”

retaining highly qualified talent in the markets where they operate. We are all familiar with the so-called "war for talent," in which it is extremely important to be able to offer a high-quality, well-equipped, employee-centered building in a central location with local transport connections—this gives you a decisive advantage. Additionally, first-class office space directly enhances productivity, which in turn has a positive impact on the bottom line.

CQ What role will art and interior design play in the design of future office spaces?

LHP I would say that our founder, my grandfather, Gerald D. Hines, had in mind office spaces that could be described as "artistic" since the inception of *Hines* in 1957. He was the only one at the time who understood that outstanding office spaces should be more than just functional buildings. That's why he worked closely with leading architects and interior designers. Together, they aimed to design office buildings that would serve as cultural landmarks and symbols of the cities in which they stood. They also wanted them to be places where everyone who interacts with them feels comfortable—both inside and out. This philosophy remains a guiding principle for our company. We always ask ourselves how we can provide the best possible experience for the people who interact with our buildings. Aesthetics, artistic expression, and design are important aspects of this. I firmly believe that this approach will prevail throughout the industry. Increasingly, our colleagues are recognizing the value of creating spaces where people enjoy spending time, whether for work, living, or cultural purposes. I believe that harnessing design and artistic sensibility in this way will shape the next generation of office spaces.

CQ One of the megatrends of our time is people's longing for a lifestyle close to nature. How will offices address this trend?

LHP I'm not at all surprised that this topic is omnipresent throughout the industry—after all, the advantages of reconnecting with nature are obvious. When we create new office spaces or renovate older ones, we carefully consider how to incorporate as much nature as possible into the interior while also creating access to the outdoors. This can range from simple greenery or indoor plants in the work areas to roof areas, terraces, and freely accessible outdoor areas. For example, we have outdoor terraces available to employees at both our global headquarters, the *Texas Tower* in Houston, and our European headquarters, the *Grainhouse* in London. Employees really enjoy using these spaces. Another advantage of focusing on closeness to nature is that our builders pay even closer attention to how a building corresponds with its immediate surroundings. If you look for ways to integrate the green spaces around the building, you will create spaces that people are drawn to and that become part of the place, no longer detached from it. It all comes down to the same key question: How do we create the best experience for all users of a space—from those who work there to the neighbors who interact with a building in different ways?

CQ How would you define the social mission of the real estate industry and architecture? And how will you fulfill it?

LHP I think my grandfather, Gerald D. Hines, put it best. He said that our company's central mission is to be unwaveringly committed to quality real estate investments, a functional built environment, better cities, and a more sustainable world.

“WE ALWAYS ASK OURSELVES HOW WE CAN PROVIDE THE BEST POSSIBLE EXPERIENCE FOR THE PEOPLE WHO INTERACT WITH OUR BUILDINGS. AESTHETICS, ARTISTIC EXPRESSION, AND DESIGN ARE IMPORTANT ASPECTS OF THIS.”

FRANÇOIS
TAUSCH

FRANÇOIS TRAUSCH
CEO and Chief Investment Officer
at PIMCO Prime Real Estate

“THE MORE WE SURROUND OURSELVES WITH TECHNOLOGY IN OUR DAILY LIVES, THE MORE BUILDINGS SHOULD APPEAL TO OUR FIVE SENSES.”

The interview with

FT François Trausch was conducted by CQ Christoph Quarch.

CQ François, some people claim that the office era is over. Do you agree?

FT The office is indeed undergoing profound change. But that doesn't mean the office is finished. It will change, just as retail did about seven years ago. I remember when the end of retail was predicted due to the rise of e-commerce, but most of it survived by adapting to the new conditions. The situation is similar to offices. The challenges they face are, of course, different, and the transformation will take place differently in various parts of the world. Offices must compete with data centers, or, in other words, with the digital cloud, which allows employees to work from anywhere. In light of this, some offices will disappear, while others will transform into spaces of interaction and collaboration.

CQ You are frequently in contact with high-profile tenants from around the world. What are the key needs and challenges of companies that will drive change in the world of work?

FT Offices are very important places for companies. Nowhere else are a company's identity and culture so visible, tangible, and experiential. That's why companies should ensure that their offices offer an attractive environment that is worth spending time in. In the US, it is said that the office must be worth the commute. That's correct. In fact, though, many offices fail to motivate people to commute voluntarily. Employees often ask themselves, with good reason, "Why should I go to the office when the workspaces there are less attractive than my apartment?" Wherever this is the case, something is wrong with the office. But what? Of course, an office is first and foremost the place where work is done. There's no getting around that. Beyond that, however, it should be a place where people meet and work together. That's precisely what you can't do when working from home. It's also important that the office is a healthy place that promotes the well-being of employees. Let me give you an example: I travel to China frequently. It never ceases to amaze me, because China is changing rapidly and, in some ways, is ahead of us. I was once in Beijing at a time when the city was still struggling with extreme air pollution. While there, I met the German architect Ole Scheeren, who built the famous CCTV building. When I entered his office, I was amazed by the incredibly fresh air. He explained to me that he had installed many air filters, which made the air quality in the offices as pure as that in the Swiss Alps. Naturally, his colleagues were more than happy to work there.

CQ I can believe that. But what about sustainability? Do you think that the offices of the future will also have to meet this criterion?

FT There's no doubt about it. Offices benefit enormously from being sustainable. Although the issue is currently weighted differently in Europe, the US, and APAC countries, it remains important for both tenants and their employees, for economic, environmental, and health reasons.

CQ It is highly likely that advanced technologies such as artificial intelligence will profoundly influence the way we work in the future. As we become increasingly surrounded by technology and digital media, it seems to me that the need for real spaces and personal encounters is growing. Could it be that people long to balance out the hype surrounding technology with environments where they can feel and touch things—where they can experience the physical presence of their colleagues?

FT People are social beings. They seek community. That may also be the reason why the metaverse is not developing as imagined. Yes, people are attracted to new technologies.

Yes, they want to use artificial intelligence. But at the end of the day, the concrete reality of real spaces is more important to them. Not only because they can touch and feel the environment, but also because real spaces have a history. That is also one of the reasons why we are renovating historic buildings.

CQ For instance?

FT In Milan, we are currently renovating a fantastic building designed by the renowned Italian architect Gio Ponti. It was formerly the headquarters of Allianz—a historic building, which is why we had to work closely with the Italian authorities responsible for monument protection. We also involved the neighbors, because we wanted to develop a plan that would meet with broad approval. But most importantly, people want to work in modern spaces that promote interaction, while also appreciating the opportunity to work in a historic building with connections to their city's past.

CQ Are there other factors besides history that determine the significance and relevance of buildings?

FT The building fabric also plays a role when it comes to creating a forward-looking environment that attracts people. For example, Europe's largest campus, located at La Défense in Paris, is being built entirely of wood. For me, this is another example of how to create a counterbalance to technology—by surrounding yourself with natural materials. Or let me put it this way: the more we surround ourselves with technology in our daily lives, the more buildings should appeal to our five senses.

CQ In addition to historical value and pleasant building materials, other factors can help create an environment where people feel at home. Art, for example, or interior design. What do you think?

“WE HAVE PROBABLY PLACED TOO MUCH EMPHASIS ON PROCESS MANAGEMENT AND TOO LITTLE ON THE COMPANY’S PURPOSE. THE CONSEQUENCES ARE OBVIOUS: PEOPLE ARE LESS MOTIVATED AND THEREFORE NOT SUFFICIENTLY EMPOWERED TO BRING ABOUT CHANGE.”

FT Good design has always made a difference. In this context, the company Vitra comes to mind. More than 50 years ago, they developed chairs that are still among the best in terms of both economy and aesthetics. But it's not just about individual objects. It's also about how objects interact with their surroundings—and how spaces interact with each other. All of this is extremely important. That's why I think interior designers have a bright future ahead of them. It's up to them to enhance the spatial experience.

CQ And what about art? Some companies have their own collections and display them in their office buildings.

FT To be honest, I don't think much of art collections in office buildings. It's a tricky subject because collecting art is a very personal thing. Whether you like it or not, a company's collection always reflects the tastes and interests of its management. This doesn't always foster a sense of belonging in the hearts of employees. On the other hand, beauty has a strong and positive influence on people. There is some truth in Dostoevsky's words that beauty will save the world. For example, I am sitting here in my Paris office. When I look out of the window, I see all these 19th-century Haussmann buildings. They are quite beautiful—beautiful in a broader sense, not only aesthetically, but also because they are both efficient and extremely sustainable. They have undergone various uses, initially as residential buildings, then as offices, and later as residential buildings again, followed by shops, and so on. Either way, I believe that the beauty of spaces and environments remains highly relevant.

CQ Beauty is inherent not only in art, but also in nature …

FT That's right, which is why proximity to nature is important. In 2023, I had the honor of chairing the jury at MIPIM, a major real estate fair that annually awards a prize for the best real estate projects in Europe. At that time, we awarded the jury's special prize to the House of Music in Budapest, designed by Japanese architect Sou Fujimoto. This building is an example of how incorporating nature can enhance a structure's beauty—and how this can give it greater significance.

CQ These days, there is a great deal of discussion about people-centered work environments. What does this concept mean to you?

FT When it comes to the work environment, we need to distinguish between the physical aspect on the one hand and the organizational form or management on the other. Good management is the most promising way to influence people. People-centered work is therefore primarily a task for a company's managers. Secondly, this approach can then be supported or complemented by the physical environment. That would be the correct order. As I said earlier, the way people work together is changing. We have probably placed too much emphasis on process management and too little on the company's purpose. The consequences are obvious: people are less motivated and therefore not sufficiently empowered to bring about change.

CQ What needs to be done?

FT In my opinion, good managers are characterized by two things. First, they make people feel like they are part of a successful team. Second, they run the company as if it were a small business. This allows them to avoid the pitfalls of large companies, such as bureaucracy and hierarchy. From this perspective, the transformation of working environments begins in the minds of managers.

CQ Leadership requires communication skills. Where these are lacking, it can cause enormous economic damage. Competent communication, on the other hand, promotes entrepreneurial thinking and creative participation. To do justice to this, architects design office spaces that look like chic lounges or lobbies. In this way, they want to create spaces where employees can engage in conversation and be creative. What do you think of these ideas?

FT In fact, many tenants want spaces that encourage collaboration. And, of course, we try to find appropriate solutions. However, we must be careful not to overdo it. It makes little sense to create spaces that resemble a kindergarten rather than a proper office. Working people still need a good desk, a comfortable chair, and a quiet environment in which to make their calls. That has to be taken care of first. It is important to strike a good balance and also to focus on the quality of the materials, interior design, and furniture ...

CQ In this book, we propose rethinking working environments with the help of a new metaphor: offices should not be seen as sterile value-creating machines, but as flourishing gardens or greenhouses. What is your view on this?

FT Why not? Of course, companies have to create value, and of course, they have to take care of product development and meet the needs of their customers. However, once these basic requirements are met, there is ample room for further development. In my mind, the working environments of the future should resemble a vertical city: a place where people not only work, but also have access to the public, allowing outsiders to access the upper floors. We recently completed a high-rise building in Berlin. It is the tallest building there. We held discussions with the city of Berlin and our development partner, EDGE, to ensure that the top floor is accessible to the public, allowing everyone to enjoy the view, not just the tenants. We also made the ground floor and parts of the first and second floors available to local residents for co-working spaces and event rooms. In a nutshell, an office building should be like a small city and have mixed use—with shops, gyms, and living space, including for students. I am convinced that all tenants will benefit from this.

CQ In Germany, there is considerable discussion about work-life balance, as if life and work were distinct areas of life. Do you think that future neighborhoods can bridge this gap?

FT To be honest, I am not a fan of the concept of work-life balance. Life takes place at work, and work is part of life. That's my view. And I firmly believe that most people can find fulfillment through their work. However, we must acknowledge that different individuals have varying ideas about where they wish to invest their creativity. For some, it's work; for others, the job is just a means to an end, allowing them to pursue their interests elsewhere. Good leadership is open to both. It will see it as its job to ensure that those who invest their energy in their work and find fulfillment in it are not shortchanged. That said, there are no limits to human capabilities. Some people flourish outside of paid work and, at the same time, thrive in their jobs. This does not have to be a contradiction. But as an employer, you can do something about it. The more you give your employees a sense of belonging, the more willing they will be to consider the hours they spend at work as *quality time*. Maybe not necessarily comparable to what they experience outside of work, but still something that has a positive impact on their lives.

CQ You have completed numerous projects. Is there one among them that embodies your personal vision of future working environments?

FT Yes, but let me start by saying that the starting point for us, real estate developers, should always be the further development of existing properties. Preserving rather than demolishing, renovating rather than rebuilding—that's important to me. Demolishing and

"LIFE IS AT WORK AND WORK IS A PART OF LIFE."

rebuilding harms the environment. It also erases the building's history. That's why we at *PIMCO Prime Real Estate* focus on transforming existing buildings into something else. We renovate and strive to repurpose the buildings we manage, making them better places. We have already discussed the Gio Ponti buildings in Milan, where we transformed outdated offices into a campus that encourages people to work together. I could cite further examples in Paris, where we have converted many Haussmann-style buildings into attractive and efficient spaces, even though the original architecture was sometimes less efficient. It may not fully compare to what they experience outside of work, but it still positively impacts their lives. When we construct new buildings, such as the aforementioned high-rise in Berlin, we implement features that are sometimes not possible in older buildings: a low carbon footprint, low energy consumption, coexistence with shops and restaurants, low-threshold access for the neighborhood, and other benefits that can only be achieved by starting from scratch.

CQ Are there specific areas that you particularly like to convert—industrial wastelands, for example?

FT Yes, certainly. But that's more a matter for urban planners and developers. As an investor, it's best to stay in the background initially. That doesn't mean, however, that we don't also undertake such projects. In New York, for example, we are about to complete the conversion of a historic warehouse—essentially a logistics center from the 1850s—into a modern, mixed-use building with offices and shops. And there will also be space for art.

CQ The conversion of unused spaces or buildings into attractive premises is more than just an investment; it is always a contribution to a larger whole: a neighborhood, a city, a region. In your opinion, what is the investor's responsibility to the local community?

FT Investors are definitely responsible for the immediate environment they create. When it comes to the municipal level, however, I believe that municipal authorities and politicians have a greater responsibility. However, private investors should always work with local communities to make the environment more attractive. Collaborating with neighbors and involving them in the project is a promising approach to ensuring that future tenants find an attractive environment where they are well received. We see this in Japan, where we developed a large logistics campus with specific consideration for local residents. It not only offers them the opportunity to work from home, but also supermarkets and restaurants that are open around the clock. This is a relatively new project that incorporates state-of-the-art structures, providing safety even in the event of an earthquake. We even included a facility that we hope will never need to be used—a local security center.

CQ In your opinion, what particularly promotes acceptance among local residents?

FT I can think of several things. Let's think back to the high-rise building in Berlin, whose top floor is accessible to everyone. Or the mixed use with shops, fitness studios, and so on, which I mentioned earlier. And then there is another issue that owners will have to deal with sooner or later: the hours of use of the workspaces. On average, offices are only used for two-thirds of the year. I think the real estate industry should ask itself what possibilities exist for use by the local population instead of simply leaving the spaces empty. However, caution is advised in such a situation, because people often do not want to share their personal spaces with others; yet, I think it's still worth considering.

LEARNING FROM GARDENS

LEARNING FROM GARDENS—Piet Oudolf, from the Netherlands, is one of the great landscape designers of our time. His magnificent gardens adorn large metropolises as well as small islands. In order to find his unmistakable style, he broke away from dogmas and cooperated with nature. A fruitful collaboration that can inspire the office districts of tomorrow.

If you want to feel the aura of the Mona Lisa, a ticket to the Louvre is a must. If you want to understand the power of Michelangelo's ceiling paintings, you should definitely visit the Sistine Chapel in Rome. The same applies to the works of Piet Oudolf. To truly appreciate the high art of the Dutchman, you have to travel like a museum visitor, getting to the bottom of it and taking the essence of it home with you. To New York, Chicago, Menorca, Amsterdam, or Somerset in England. None of these places may be exactly around the corner. But Oudolf fans know that his large-format works can also be viewed in the middle of Germany—in the place where you would least expect it: Hamm. In the eastern Ruhr region, they are spread over 7,000 square meters on a former coal mine site between the A1 and A2. Oudolf arranged three natural works of art in 2010, 2011, and 2019, where a state garden expo *(Landesgartenschau)* was held in 1984. Narrow paths lead visitors through the middle and confront them at every turn with the main characters—agrimony and vernonia, aster and elecampane, Cambridge milk parsley and silver primrose. Fifty thousand perennials from around 70 different species have been planted here. They do not impress with their spectacular bright colors, but with their understated elegance. They are not neatly arranged in rows but suggest a wilderness. In fact, it is a planned wilderness.

This alone shows that Oudolf's principle cannot be reconciled with the tradition of European stately parks and gardens. His works of art are not mere decoration, they are not subject to a strict rhythm, they do not reach their peak in summer, and they are not destroyed after each flowering season. The man from Hummelo works with perennial flowering groups of plants, which he places in direct connection with each other as in a collage, and whose communities he repeatedly takes up in the overall area. There is no single focus on which the eye could rest for longer, like the face of the Mona Lisa or da Vinci's fingers pointing at each other in the creation of Adam. The viewer's gaze is constantly drawn onwards. Oudolf composes in structural categories of change, repetition, duration, harmony, and, last but not least, sensuality and atmosphere. According to Oudolf, he does not have a philosophy in the true sense of the word. He simply wants to share his passion with people by creating spaces that give pleasure. "Good gardens transport you," he says. "They are very emotional." That is why he has never been primarily concerned with conveying nature in the style of a biologist, "but rather the feeling that nature creates." Sometimes, according to Oudolf, the beauty of nature is so strong that it can hardly be explained. He has been playing with this

“MY DESIGNS HAVE A ROMANTIC, SENSITIVE AURA, BUT I ALSO FIND THE WILD AND SPONTANEOUS VERY IMPORTANT.”

effect ever since he began to learn from nature and distance himself from the dogmas of English gardening manuals. He reduced human control of plant growth as much as possible. He created landscapes within landscapes that constantly change with the seasons and exude beauty even when they have faded. He staged an incomparable open-air theater whose protagonists appear in different guises with each visit and, precisely for this reason, always inspire different emotions in the viewer.

This is exactly what we can learn for arranging working environments. If we break away from guidelines that someone else once considered sensible and allow ourselves more freedom, we can design spaces and neighborhoods in which we can think more freely, develop our latent potential, and generate new growth. If we let go a little, relinquish control, and trust in the self-organization of the system, we will certainly get different results than before. If we stage these new spaces in a diverse way and form communities within this diversity, opportunities for cooperation arise that strengthen vitality and resilience. The inner cohesion in such a place automatically fulfills the basic human need for protection and security. If all of this is also created in an aesthetic environment whose beauty is authentic and not just a façade, we create a unique quality of stay that allows us to work in a joyful atmosphere.

But is it enough to simply transfer the *lessons* of an Oudolf-style garden to the architecture of office districts in the New Work era? The Dutchman is convinced that there is now more to sustainable building than simply taking nature as an orientation, namely, making nature itself a component. “Architects today (...) are expected to take nature into account in their designs,” he says. “Our awareness of the environment has increased. That’s why gardens have become so important.” People want more greenery and accept more wilderness as long as it is aesthetically pleasing. If nature looked like “Wow!,” people would no longer throw their garbage into it.

It is worth taking a closer look at the path of the person who makes such a statement and can reliably create this “Wow!” effect. Piet Oudolf was born in Haarlem, the Netherlands, in 1944. He was not someone who found his destiny in his early years, but first had to earn his living as a waiter, bartender, fishmonger, and steelworker before he acquired a taste for it in a garden center shortly after his 25th birthday. He worked there as a Christmas tree salesman and was asked if he would like to work in the nursery. He enjoyed it so much that he decided to go to night school to gain qualifications that would enable him to set up

his own garden design company. His passion for plants grew, and he traveled to England, visiting parks, gardens, and nurseries, where he found inspiration and collected every plant he liked. “I was obsessed with it,” he says. “But nature wasn’t the main focus; it was the decorative value of plants. I thought in terms of beauty and asked myself: how can I arrange plants as personalities in such a way that they create a beautiful picture?” He didn’t have a garden of his own, so he planted his secret imports in the garden of his mother’s restaurant.

A major turning point for Oudolf was the move from Haarlem to the countryside, where, together with his wife, he was able to try out in experimental gardens exactly which plant personalities he was dealing with and under which circumstances they could get along with each other. Ultimately, this constant research work became the secret of his success. A deep knowledge of plants is the basis, he says, and gardeners should invest more time in getting to know plants. “Plants will disappoint you if you don’t know them,” explains Oudolf. “It takes years to understand plants and know how to use them. They are like human beings.”

Encounters with people from both the Native Plant Movement (which advocates eliminating invasive species in favor of regional flora) and the New Perennial Movement (which promotes garden design based on the wildness of nature) prompted Oudolf to abandon the previous rules of gardening for purely decorative purposes. The English had made him too dependent on their textbooks and calendars, which told him exactly what to do with which plants and when. From then on, he used wild and native plants, above all perennials and ornamental grasses. They make up around 70 percent of each of his gardens. Oudolf’s gardens are now more reminiscent of the prairie from *Winnetou* films than the manicured borders from *Miss Marple* classics. Although Oudolf always referred to leading figures who had inspired him—such as Karl Foerster, Wolfgang Oehme, or Henk Gerritsen—in the 1990s, he himself rose to become a leading figure in natural garden design, setting a milestone with his first book *Dream Plants for the Natural Garden* in 2000 and being appointed to ever more illustrious projects.

Probably the most spectacular is his cultivation of the *High Line*—a former elevated railway line in Manhattan—in 2009. In doing so, he has succeeded in creating new attractions, even in places that are primarily known for monstrous, brutalist architecture. With over

“I DISCOVER BEAUTY IN THINGS THAT ARE NOT BEAUTIFUL AT FIRST GLANCE. IT IS THE JOURNEY OF LIFE TO FIND OUT WHAT TRUE BEAUTY IS AND TO REALIZE THAT IT IS EVERYWHERE.”

eight million visitors annually, the *High Line* has become the most popular destination for tourists in New York. Not only does this reveal a great deal about the megatrend of sustainability, it also shows a great deal about people's longing for an unspoiled world as an alternative to the ongoing obsession with paving our cities. We can also take this with us on the way to life-friendly working quarters: not to abuse nature as an ornament, but to reintegrate it into our everyday urban life on a larger scale. In Manhattan, in Amsterdam, or Hamm. Piet Oudolf once said that people can create their own worlds with gardens, "but nature is the biggest garden we have, and that's why we have to protect it."

NEIGHBOR-HOODS FOR THE FUTURE

THE ROLE MODELS—The peculiarity of life on earth is that it has produced a highly diverse spectrum of species, cultures, traditions, and aesthetics. However, if we examine global efforts to develop architectural solutions for future-proof workplaces, current ideas are moving in very similar directions. Whether in Southeast Asia, Europe, or North America, the respective legacies of previous generations are being (re)designed in such a way that the vital connections to nature and people are reconstituted.

URBAN FARMING OFFICE
HO CHI MINH CITY, VIETNAM
VTN ARCHITECTS

The Urban Farming Office in Ho Chi Minh City doesn't resemble an office building from the outside—neither at first glance nor even at second glance. Like a densely overgrown rock, it reaches for the sky in all the shades of green that nature has to offer, and you wouldn't be surprised if a few langurs suddenly jumped out of the thicket. But behind the jungle-like façade is a glass front, fitted into a concrete skeleton. Inside, on a 300-square-meter floor area and five airy floors, people sit at long wooden tables in front of their computers, hold conferences, or relax with green tea. They, too, will be surprised every day, because even from the inside, this workplace does not resemble traditional office space. You feel like you're in a cave, safe, protected, and cooled. The leafy green, which makes the sun's rays shine in, has a calming effect. The view through the window front immediately shows how the architects have succeeded in creating this magic: The plants were mounted on metal struts in front of the façade in flexible box modules, some large, some small, some shallow, some deep.

The future belongs to eco-expressive buildings like these, especially in places like this. Urbanization in Vietnam is progressing rapidly. Today, 40 percent of the more than 100 million inhabitants live in urban areas. In Ho Chi Minh City alone, in the subtropical south of the country, there are nine million. For many years, dynamic economic growth has meant that nature is being pushed back, traffic volumes are increasing, the air is deteriorating, and the increasingly sealed metropolitan areas are becoming less resilient to extreme weather events, such as heatwaves and flooding.

The Urban Farming Office aims to provide a solution to these challenging megatrends, which are intensifying unevenly in our cities in many respects. The green façade and roof garden not only have a positive effect on the microclimate inside and in the immediate vicinity, but also filter the air, provide habitats for insects and birds, reduce energy costs, and invite people to harvest. The plants, which are irrigated with stored rainwater, consist mainly of native fruit trees, herbs, and vegetables, thus contributing to local food security. But an omnipotent architectural statement alone cannot save an overburdened city. As a beacon, however, it can encourage imitators and force the realization that there is hardly a better alternative than bringing nature back into the neighborhoods.

RATP HABITAT HEADQUARTERS
PARIS, FRANCE
ATELIER DU PONT

How do you create a feel-good object of New Work architecture in the middle of a densely built-up Parisian district when there is actually no reasonable space left? How do you do it when you want to bring nature on board, but there are only a few trees around as decoration? So, what do you do if you want to integrate precisely these two points—coziness and closeness to nature—into the DNA of the new building? You have to get inventive, of course. Especially as the architects from Atelier du Pont had to accomplish this feat in a corner under which an underground parking garage had already been dug into the ground.

And yet it stands today, the headquarters of the French real estate company RATP Habitat, in this backyard of Rue Bagnolet, not far from the Père Lachaise cemetery. Due to the conditions and the architects' aspirations, wood was chosen as the defining material. Wooden frames support the three floors, wooden parquet covers the concrete floors, wooden slats adorn the ceilings and walls, the movable room dividers are made of wood, a tree stylized with wooden beams stretches upwards in the chill zone of the atrium, wooden furniture suggests a relaxed living room atmosphere, and in the outdoor area, wide wooden stairs, wooden paths, and wooden terraces connect the different working levels in the style of a sweeping slalom run. Everywhere and again and again: plants. Trees, shrubs, flower beds, flowers, grasses.

The light-flooded interior areas have deliberately broken with traditional office structures reminiscent of barracks or battery cages. There is even talk of disruption here. The focus was on spatial flexibility, expandability, and multiple uses. This is symbolized by the movable walls, which, in combination with wooden pillars, sometimes create small, discreet chambers, while at other times they create spaciousness. Probably the most curious features, however, can be found outside on the terraces: Glass greenhouses lure employees outside. However, it is not tomatoes that grow in them, but thoughts, visions, and plans. Even in rainy weather, teams can hold meetings under the Parisian sky, or inspiration can be born on its own. Can you work more beautifully? You just have to be prepared to be observed in this kind of greenhouse effect.

PONCE CITY MARKET
ATLANTA, USA
NIMMONS, CARR AND WRIGHT

PONCE CITY MARKET

Anyone visiting Ponce City Market in the east of Atlanta today can hardly imagine that this place was once an idyllic recreational area. Around 160 years ago, the citizens of the still young city in the Ponce de Leon Springs region used to relax here. It was named after the Spanish explorer Juan Ponce de León, who is said to have searched for the Fountain of Youth between his conquests. At the turn of the century, the area was transformed into an amusement park, and a little later, the lake was drained, and a sports arena was also built in its place. Eternal youth? That still somehow fits. When people ran out of fun in the mid-1920s, the Chicago-based retail company Sears, Roebuck & Co. acquired the land and built an imposing brick department store on it, which was subsequently expanded several times. Today, one hundred years later, it is precisely this complex where you can once again shop, dine, live, work, and, yes, even have fun, as a few attractions have been installed on the roof in remembrance of the amusement park. Carrying a historic building into the future undoubtedly involves responsibility. But it also requires creativity to harmonize the old with the needs of the present. This has been achieved in a remarkable way here.

But until then, the complex was subject to other influences. In the 1990s, for example, Sears, Roebuck & Co. moved out, the mall declined, many stores relocated, and less than ten percent of the building remained in use. Subsequently, the Atlanta City Council used it as a branch office. To revitalize the entire area, the municipality found a partner: Jamestown acquired the property in 2011 and initiated a multi-year redevelopment to make it available for new purposes. Since 2015, Ponce City Market has garnered international attention as a showcase project for both adaptive reuse and the revitalization of historic architecture.

It has become a much-visited centerpiece of Atlanta, offering lavish retail space around the central food hall, offices for innovative companies, and loft-style residences on a total of 1.2 million square meters. With public parks and direct access to the Atlanta Beltline, Ponce City Market has become another iconic destination for tourists. The city, known for its civil rights and soul music, has also become a hotspot for urban development. In 2024, Ponce City Market welcomed 3.6 million visitors. Speaking for the residents of the attraction, you could say that Ponce City Market is now their village! All trades and amenities are conveniently close together, embedded in a green network of paths. Without a good reason, you would never want to leave the neighborhood. The locals now proudly refer to it as the "New Atlanta."

And there is no end in sight. A success like this inevitably sparks new ambitions. In 2024, an additional 700,000 square meters of residential, restaurant, office, and retail space were completed in the area around the historic Ponce City Market complex. These include a sustainably designed and constructed solid timber building that utilizes native Georgia-grown yellow pine, resulting in a significantly lower carbon footprint and a supply chain that is regionally focused. This includes the Signal House, a residential building designed for a sophisticated urban lifestyle, making every day "frictionless" and "seamless." This means offering the ultimate in both technical and human services—from digital networking and ongoing IT support to social events such as communal dinners. The second development phase of the Signal House includes Scout Living, which incorporates aspects of assisted living and hospital-like services into everyday life, offering very flexible rental periods ranging from a single night to a year.

Whatever the next chapter may be, it will certainly tie in with the long history of a city that looks to the future while always remembering its roots.

THIS WAY TO
ROOF
FOOD HALL
SHOPS
OFFICES

ARKET

STRATOSFERICA
TURIN, ITALY

Torinostratosferica
HERMADA CAPOLINEA

The interview with

LB Luca Ballarini,
founder and director of Stratosferica,
was conducted by

CQ Christoph Quarch.

CQ Luca, I found a quote in one of your presentations that really impressed me: "Everyone is a place maker." What led you to this belief, and how does it affect your work?

LB This sentence is inspired by the first lines of Norman Potter's 1968 book *What Is a Designer*.[19] Ever since I read this book, the words "Everyone is a designer" have stayed with me. Potter was not saying that everyone should be able to earn a living through professional design. Instead, he meant that everyone has the ability to focus on specific goals, to orient their actions and define steps—in short, to design a process. Because if we have defined our goals, we can also achieve them. And if we fail, we have the chance to do better next time. However, our phrase "Everyone is a place maker" is not just praise of human creativity, but also an incentive to take action. We want to convey to people that they not only have the ability but also the duty to participate in shaping places.

CQ What exactly do you mean by place making?

LB For me, place making means understanding, shaping, and organizing our relationship with a place. We can transform a place into an environment that is meaningful for us, our work, and our relationships. With this in mind, we want to take action and show that everyone can be a place maker.

CQ Is this an invitation to your project partners to discover their undiscovered creative abilities?

LB Yes, it is an invitation. The great thing is that we are continually improving at convincing people to put our ideas and visions into practice. I believe that our mission is to educate people about the purpose and value of designing spaces, transforming and revitalizing them.

CQ How do you proceed with this revitalization?

LB We start from an existing scenario. There is always potential lying dormant that needs to be developed. However, our aim is not only to make this potential visible, but also to bring the hidden value to light. So we focus on this other, still hidden reality. We visualize it and consider how we can bring it to life through creation and design. To achieve this, it is essential to align our partners with these values and visions, as the future reality is akin to a fruit that requires fertilization before it can be harvested. This succeeds when others understand our vision and connect it with their own imagination. Only then can they grasp its deeper meaning. Only when this is the case can we create something together and work together successfully. When I look back on my career, I realize that it has always been collaboration that has moved me forward. As a student, I once took on the challenge of producing a magazine—a task that required more than one person. Since then, everything I've done has been in collaboration with others. Especially when it comes to place making, it's essential to bring together a diverse group of people and stakeholders, including both private and public entities, to share their unique perspectives.

CQ You enjoy working with young people. Why is that?

LB We give the young people who work with us the opportunity to try something outside their everyday routines and away from their duties as students or pupils: something they enjoy, something where they learn, and at the same time, have intensive experiences, especially social experiences. Because that is what they long for most: Community, togetherness, that is their real motive, even when they go to bars or celebrate their parties. That's what excites them. And it is precisely this enthusiasm that is important. We want them to be enthusiastic about what they do. That's why we invite them to do what excites us. We share our own desires and wishes with them, and in return, we get their enthusiasm and passion.

CQ What does that look like, exactly?

LB First and foremost, it is essential to us that young people understand what motivates us. This is the only way they can find out whether they share our goals: whether they also want to improve public spaces, claim them for themselves, take care of urban areas, and revitalize neglected places or districts.

CQ What is your experience of this?

LB Most young people share our goals. They correspond to their attitude to life. But that alone is not enough. It is crucial that they experience themselves as agents of change and that they can learn something through their actions. We want them to experience that they can make a difference with their own hands, something they can feel and see with their own eyes, even if it's just a chair or a bench. It all inspires them—whether they are budding designers, architects, urban planners, or whatever. It's a real, felt experience that they have in a public space, not in a university classroom, and that accompanies them throughout the whole process, from the first drawing to the execution.

CQ Okay, the young people you work with benefit from this. But what do you get out of it?

LB Through our collaboration with students, our network gets bigger and bigger. Our young partners are the citizens of tomorrow. And not only that: they are also the designers, urban planners, and architects of tomorrow. Doing things together unites us. We have the same values and visions, and we have a similar mindset. This enables us to spread our philosophy and our message. To put it in a nutshell: our partners are like sparks that are ignited by our enthusiasm and which they then spread to their surroundings in their own way.

CQ Let's stay with your philosophy for a moment, focusing on the mission of your company, *Stratosferica*. You are concerned with combining ecological, social, and cultural aspects. How do these factors combine to form a theory of future urban spaces?

LB Our theory of place making, the development of urban spaces, rests on two pillars. Firstly: *imagination*. This is something that has been criminally neglected by modern urban development. Instead of imagining spaces worth living in, the focus has been on purely practical and functional aspects. We, on the other hand, say that cities are mental weapons—weapons in a non-aggressive but humane sense. For as long as they have existed—i.e., for around 10,000 years—they have been manifestations of our relationship to the cosmos. Or let's put it this way: they are man's response to the cosmos, a response with which he expresses how he locates himself in the cosmos, how he wants to leave his mark on the earth, and what meaning he wants to give himself and his surroundings. Seen in this way, our cities are always an expression of the power we have gained over nature. We use them to subjugate nature and create something of our own, something that resists nature, the manifestation of an *imago mundi* in which we are connected to one another. Everything we create is a product of our imagination. It is always first imagined, then designed, then built, then experienced, and finally told. Places, therefore, never stand on their own, but are surrounded by stories. They not only have a history, they are stories. Understanding these stories is essential for the development of spaces.

CQ You spoke of two pillars of your theory.

LB That's right. Cities are not only a product of our imagination and narrative, but they are also our *destination*. Life is increasingly shifting to urban spaces. We build cities, we live in cities. We are becoming an urban species. Cities as *imagination* and *destination*: this is the foundation of our theory and the basis of our work. We aim to harness the power of imagination in the development of cities. We take people's longing for connection and community seriously and are aware that we are physical beings who interact with our surroundings. We know that we will succeed best if we allow local people to participate and collaborate in the improvement, and that applies to each of the three areas you mentioned: Culture, Ecology, and Social.

CQ We've discussed the social aspect of your work. How do you deal with the ecological challenges of urban spaces?

LB Environmental problems are the biggest challenge we face. We know that we must prevent the global average temperature from rising by more than 1.5 degrees Celsius. However, we also recognize the need for global solutions. There is little we can do regionally or locally. That doesn't stop us from doing what little we can by using environmentally friendly materials and choosing sustainable processes. But all in all, our options are very limited.

CQ Let's then discuss the importance of culture in urban development.

LB Culture is conveyed through language and communication. When it comes to inspiring cultural change, it is important to start with people's communication habits. At *Stratosferica*, we therefore see ourselves as communication designers who create spaces for partnership and transparent exchange between people.

CQ We have already mentioned that cities reveal something of how people position themselves in relation to nature and the cosmos. The ancient Greek word *kósmos* literally means *beautiful order*. Accordingly, the ancients believed that a city was only a good city if it reflected the beauty of the cosmos. What role does beauty play in your philosophy of place making?

LB If you wander through a large city today, it is difficult to discover beauty anywhere. This is because architecture and urban development are not oriented towards beauty, but towards functionality. Everything that people build and design today must serve to satisfy immediate needs. It's always about efficiency: in housing, in transportation, even in recreation. As a result, our cities resemble machines that care little for values such as beauty or humanity. For those of us who want to develop cities and their surroundings into better spaces worth living in, beauty plays an important role. However, it is not easy to do it justice.

CQ What is the problem?

LB If we want to create larger green spaces in a neighborhood, for example, the question of safety immediately arises. For many people, safety is more important than beauty. But that's not all: people's ideas of what beauty is can also be very different. Some people think of something shiny or luxurious. But that's not what we mean. We are not interested in creating the perfect city or the perfect neighborhood. We want to improve the real places here and now. We are not interested in a *U-topia*, a non-place, but in an *Eu-topia*, a good place. As a desirable goal, beauty is not a utopian, but an eutopian quality of urban spaces.

CQ Are you saying that you are primarily interested in discovering and revealing existing beauty?

LB That's how it is. Every place has its own genius loci, its own special spirit, its own special meaning. Discovering it and staging it are the decisive factors, utilizing our senses to feel and work out the possibilities inherent in a place. This is how real transformation happens. And this is how a higher kind of beauty can be realized. We don't need a general beautification of individual aspects of a city. We need concrete improvements in a specific place for the people who live there.

CQ This is an expanded understanding of beauty. Beauty is not only something aesthetically appealing, but also beauty in the sense of harmony between place and people, beauty as a meaningful and meaningful response to the factual conditions of a place …

LB Yes, beauty is the meaning that people can understand in a place. This also includes its value and usefulness. The material and the spiritual play together in the beauty of a place. It is also important to me that we bring this spiritual side to the forefront once again. Otherwise, we will end up with cities that are perhaps still prettied up for the sake of utility, but are otherwise just used and consumed. This then leads to overtourism and a brutal exploitation of all resources. Or it leads to insecurity and crime. Either way, all of this plunges the people who live in these cities into misery.

CQ What's behind this dynamic?

LB Today, we no longer typically interpret cities as places of human life, but rather as machines for satisfying needs. The reason for this is that we first banished the spiritual dimension from our minds and then from our cities. But that is wrong, because it denies the human. That is what we are fighting against. And it is perhaps the most beautiful result of our place making processes that people are realizing it is possible to make run-down places more human. It is possible to revitalize these places and bring out their forgotten spiritual dimension anew through good design and attentive care. The result may not be the great universal beauty of the philosophers. Still, it is a small beauty that can be delivered like a package to a specific place at a specific time—accurately, precisely, and originally, and so authentically that people can perceive it and resonate with it. If this is successful, they can reconnect with the meaning behind it.

> **CQ** How would it be if, in the future, we were to orient ourselves in the development of districts and cities not on the metaphor of the machine, but on the model of the garden, a living system that requires holistic cultivation and not one-dimensional linear optimization?

LB I like the image of the garden. And I like the idea that we, as urban planners, are less like engineers and more like gardeners, bringing new life to derelict spaces and run-down corners to transform them into places where people enjoy spending time. This brings to mind some thoughts I came across in a poignant letter from Scottish biologist, scientist, and urban planner Patrick Geddes[20] to his children. He explains why gardens are places that can teach us all about the organization and evolution of life, and how and why we need to care for our environment. Geddes was convinced that cities are living organisms that can only be approached appropriately with a holistic way of thinking, and that one must always see the whole first and then the individual. Geddes, by the way, is the author of the famous formula “Think global—act local” and the originator of many other important ideas that we draw on in our work. Since I have been intensively involved with his work, the garden as a symbol of a living organism in which everything interacts with everything else has been just as omnipresent in my thinking as the idea that we should behave like careful gardeners in all our planning and actions. Today, it is of utmost importance that we not only discuss nature conservation superficially but also truly recognize the depth of our connection to nature.

HAMBURG DECKS
HAMBURG, GERMANY
STEIDLE ARCHITECTS, KIESSLER ARCHITECTS

brand

When the former publishing giant Gruner + Jahr started looking for a plot of land at the end of the 1970s to respond to its expanding press portfolio with a new building, its attention eventually fell on a 22,000-square-meter plot of rubble between St. Michael's Church and the harbor, one of the last open wounds of the Second World War. The owner was the City of Hamburg, but it had other plans and wanted to have access to another Elbe Tunnel dug right there. In 1982, common sense prevailed in the Senate, and after a multi-stage architectural competition, the vision of a press building unlike any other was presented in 1984.

The Munich-based creative minds at Steidle + Partner and Kiessler Architects were the most precise in their response to the client's wish not to build a simple office building on the promenade, but an entire quarter, a city within the city. More precisely: a newspaper city.

It was to exude the very essence of a free press—openness, transparency, exchange, encounters. All of this is staged with its own architectural self-confidence, yet still oriented towards architectural quotes from the neighborhood, including the harbor on one hand, and the narrow streets of the Portuguese quarter on the other. It was not until 1990 that the result emerged. Like an ocean liner made of glass, steel, and wood that had been washed ashore and then raised, with huge portholes and hundreds of meters of railing, a lookout at lofty heights, and massive chimneys, there it stood, the ultimate publishing house of the future.

The interior was not dominated by the darkness of an oil tanker, but by the brightness of a greenhouse. In fact, every floor, every corner, every corridor, every desk where the stories for the many magazines were conceived and written could be reached by sunlight as planned. Long corridors with light wooden floors, few elevators, and many stairs promoted not only communication but also the fitness of the workers; the hall-like canteen, in which trees grew, comparable to a generously designed menagerie, became not an interchangeable eating hall, but a popular place with which one could even impress editorial guests.

All of this shaped the daily lives of many generations of journalists, but one thing had been missing the whole time: access for the population and the streams of tourists moving along the Elbe and up to the Michel. This had actually been part of the original plan. People were supposed to be able to walk back and forth through the newspaper city on the first floor. Stores and cafés were to line the edges of the building, inviting people to linger. Things turned out differently. It was probably security concerns that ultimately led to the Quarter for All becoming an unusual but hermetically sealed building complex with a main entrance, two narrow revolving doors, and strict controls at reception. The desired liveliness prevailed above all inside. Those who did not work here were only allowed to look at the shell.

Now, 35 years later, the publishing house was dwarfed and scattered to the four winds due to the rapid transformation of media—precisely this forgotten element of the greatest possible publicity is moving into this building. And curiously enough, it is once again the people from Steidle and Kiessler who oversee it. "We are reinterpreting the old idea of opening up the building to people," says architect Johann Spengler. To this end, the first floor, with its double-story height, will be made accessible so that it can be traversed from all directions. But why should you do that? A new attraction is moving in that was previously missing from the tourist core area of the Port of Hamburg: a classic market hall. One third of the lower 8,000 square meters will permanently house the stalls of a high-quality weekly market. At the same time, the inner area will attract visitors with a variety of gastronomic offerings. "Rough, like the Chelsea Market in New York" is how the real estate developers at Tishman Speyer—who are also involved in the major Hamburg project—envision it.

Above the market, 50,000 square meters of office space for various tenants will be spread across the remaining three floors. Their employees will no longer be able to experience the benefits of light-filled workplaces exclusively in single or double offices, as was previously the case—something that no investor or tenant can sell these days—but in even more airy open-plan arrangements without the dividing walls. The architects and developers were unable to implement the open New Work aesthetic in every aspect of the former publishing house's evolution. The compromise with the historic-monument preservation authority provides for areas in which the original closed corridors with the outgoing individual offices will be preserved.

Despite all the claims of wanting to create a new Hamburg attraction with the open market situation, tenants and employees alone will find an exclusive feature just a few meters above the office ceilings—in the former management tower. Up there, a 360-degree bar is now set to crown the busy days, perhaps following a yoga session or workout in the communal areas below. After all, the real estate developers also need to take this to heart: The younger generations, who have grown fond of working from home during the coronavirus pandemic, will not be brought back to the office with the argument that a German publishing giant once made headlines here. The offers of office space designed for communication, a trendy market hall, integrated fitness facilities, and a few drinks with a premium view of the *Elbphilharmonie* are probably more convincing.

Perhaps one or two people will even come up with the idea of living in the immediate vicinity. That will also be possible. In front of the old publishing house, where the dreary employee parking lot once stood, an apartment block with 112 apartments will bring further vitality to the area in the future. This is another way of reviving the original character of the neighborhood, which never truly materialized. Wooden decks will create a link between the residential development and the office and market buildings. The campus will be complemented by a five-story cube, primarily made of glass and wood, in which everything associated with New Work today will be found. The architects from the Norwegian firm Snøhetta are responsible for this. The cube will deliberately call itself a "new office building," even if at first glance it has little in common with the old office buildings that are typical of the Elbe riverside inner-city location. Like the Kontorhaus Stubbenhuk, for instance, a mighty and richly decorated colossus in the brick expressionist style, just a few meters away, which is also part of the reactivated ensemble. Built around 100 years ago, it housed a grain merchant, a shipping company, and the Henri Nannen School of Journalism, among others. After restoration by Tishman Speyer, it was handed over to a new owner—the family-owned company Wempe—in 2025. Workshops, a marketing department, and a museum are moving into the watch manufacturer and jeweler's second Hamburg location. A clear commitment to the hometown. Just as the entire development project feels like a clear commitment to the Free and Hanseatic City of Hamburg.

BREWERY
MARKT
cuisine
cuisine

THE CAMPUS
TOKYO, JAPAN
KOKUYO ARCHITECTS

MPUS

What is an office? "An office is a place where a company gathers its employees to do business." And what is a campus? "The campus is a place where people voluntarily gather to expand their experiences and connections." This is the contrast with which the designers of the Japanese furniture brand Kokuyo refer to the special feature of their flagship project, "The Campus," in the heart of Tokyo. Rather than spending time in isolation completing immediate tasks in a traditional office, they believe in the value of individuals acquiring knowledge, being inspired, adopting different perspectives, forging new relationships, and experiencing personal fulfillment while contributing to the missions of others in a highly diverse new work environment—all during working hours.

The floors of two former office buildings have been gutted and furnished in entirely different ways to achieve this desired effect and as a countertrend to isolation in mainstream hamster wheels. There is a floor called the "Gather Floor," for instance, which is intended for in-depth debates. The teams that book in there can adapt the design of this area to their individual needs and even move the walls. The "Nurture Floor" aims to promote both personal and organizational growth by fostering dialogue between top management and employees. The "Progress Floor" offers an environment that is difficult to replicate while working from home. It is equipped with first-class equipment and furniture, including personal workspaces. In this environment, with its rather monotonous design and limited distractions, employees can concentrate and immerse themselves fully in their work.

Floors with public areas, which make up almost exactly 50 percent of the space, are available to both regular customers and the neighborhood. The focus here is on out-of-the-box experiences, exchanges with people from other companies or completely different parts of society. To make these encounters possible, connecting paths were created between the two buildings, leading from the street area up to the recreational levels, and offering numerous green spaces.

By opening up to the outside world, providing creative spaces for leisure activities, and organizing flea markets, the campus has become a new center of the district since 2021, something that would never have been achieved by using it solely as an office space. Over the past three years, 200,000 people have found their way here, and more than 90 collaborative events with companies or universities have taken place. In addition to social sustainability, ecological sustainability also played a significant role in the transformation. For example, the central intentions were to reduce dependence on plastics throughout the entire building operation, to enhance the neighborhood's resilience to extreme weather by using infiltration-capable aerated concrete paving, and to use renewable energy sources to supply the campus predominantly.

LA FORGIATURA
MILAN, ITALY
GIUSEPPE TORTATO ARCHITETTI

Medtronic
3,5 t

Quando la città cambia tu guarda i suoi colori. When a city changes, you see it in its colors. This is roughly how you could translate the title of the mural that has become a 57-meter-long calling card for Milan's Certosa neighborhood. It features visual quotes from past industrial architecture, broken down into geometric shapes in a reduced color palette of blue, black, gray, yellow, orange, and a hint of green. Stairs, tunnels, cranes, railroads, factory halls, and streets are alluded to, wildly pushed into one another and stretched out so far that you can't help but think of the Berlin Wall. It is an abstract narrative of the decades-long identity of this extremely dense former steel site in the northwest of the Italian metropolis, surrounded by many streets. Created in 2022 as part of a design festival, the color work by graphic design studio CamuffoLab seems to shout: "Come in! Look behind the wall!" That was probably the intention, as the La Forgiatura corporate campus is located here, named after the local forge that once specialized in producing special steel components.

The architecture, which still retains a brutalist feel, has been brought into the 21st century, with elements supplemented, reduced, and continually refined. Innovative companies from the international medical, fashion, and IT sectors, in particular, have moved into the multifunctional center, which also features the branch of the former steel manufacturer. Eight buildings, whose façades are dominated by steel and glass, are held together by a geometric network of paths that repeatedly create green, hilly islands. The former, elongated factory halls in particular give a sense of their former use. Openly acknowledging their history, they are referred to as *Meccanica* (mechanics), *Uffici* (offices), or *Tempra* (temperature control). The 100,000 square meters are also reserved for visual arts and music, which are clearly not token areas: Spacious exhibition rooms and event venues regularly attract creative people to Certosa.

The restaurants do the same for the hungry. The transformed neighborhood is also a great gastronomic experiment. Of course, Italian cuisine does not need to hide from anyone, but the culinary scenes of New York, Copenhagen, and Paris have certainly inspired Certosa. The deliberately dense placement of high-quality restaurants is intended to foster a community of those who appreciate the quality and sustainability of the ingredients. This also means the guests who come and go, but above all, the chefs, traders, and producers who work or deliver there every day. They should be able to meet like-minded people and spur them on to top performance in order to turn this corner of Milan into a hotspot that can easily compete with New York, Copenhagen, and Paris. Because when a city changes, you can tell by its taste. Quando la città cambia tu guarda il suo gusto.

This is all part of a larger urban development plan that is being driven forward in the northwest of the Lombard metropolis. The Certosa neighborhood was never in danger of being seen as a kind of building container and only being refurbished here and there with the help of a few architectural highlights. From the very beginning of the transformation, it was interpreted as a space for experience that is oriented towards the needs of the people who live and work in it, as an integrated, multifunctional hub that attempts to create a balance between quality of life, accessibility, and sustainability. "Cultural landscape of well-being" is perhaps what we could call it today. The drivers behind this were not a few new skyscrapers or transportation axes, but the soft triad of culinary delights, music, and art, carefully staged between historic and contemporary buildings, between reactivation and innovation, between memory and the future. Such a district pulsates; it lives automatically. It attracts people. It lets people linger. It does not impose itself on them, but invites them to discover its diversity piece by piece.

CROSTA
loste café

THE LENBACHGÄRTEN OFFICES
MUNICH, GERMANY
HILMER, SATTLER, ALBRECHT AND STEIDLE ARCHITECTS

To really understand what the future of Munich's *Lenbachgärten* will look like, it is worth taking a moment to look back on this neighborhood's past. When its namesake, the painter Franz von Lenbach, was at the height of his creative powers—specifically, at the turn of the century before last—gardens had a special function. On the one hand, they were intended to extend the living space into the outside, to integrate the recreational aspect of greenery, and to refresh the soul; on the other hand, even then, they were regarded as an essential natural counterweight in the expanding urban spaces, enabling people to meet in a relaxed atmosphere. In Munich at the time, landscape architect Max Kolb was the leading proponent of this principle, and he dared to denounce the loss of undeveloped areas publicly. People listened to him! He was commissioned to design residential green spaces, large Munich parks, and squares that are still characteristic today. He also planned the garden of the Tuscan-style *Lenbachhaus*.

Today, a five-minute walk away, the *Lenbachgärten* spreads out on the edge of the Old Botanical Gardens, a bright, high-end ensemble of seven buildings with work, residential, and hotel functions that was completed in 2007. Since the office buildings on the site, the *Lenbachgärten Offices*, with an area of 30,000 square meters, found a new owner in 2019: in the pension fund of the energy supplier E.ON, work has been underway not only on reviving the basic function of the garden, but also to use architectural finesse to encourage the entire office complex to create a greater sense of community. The aim is to turn a working quarter into a collaborative one.

Let's start with the gardens, the green spaces that previously lay over the offices as conventional ground cover and had few ecological and no social components. In the course of upgrading the quarter, the roofs are to receive a considerable boost. A park-like arrangement of trees, shrubs, hedges, perennials, and grasses is planned in line with the desire for the greatest possible diversity for the largest possible number of insects, which is by no means just a home for honeybees. Although they are supposed to produce honey up there in their own hive, they are supposed to share the new terrain with many insects that do not visit flowers. The more diverse the roofs are, the more stable and resilient the ecosystems that grow on them become, offering greater compensation in extreme weather conditions and shaping the microclimate far beyond the roof itself. If such roofs are also made accessible to people, with elevators and stairs leading to them, and if seating invites people to linger, not only for the employees of the resident companies but also for people from the neighborhood, then a roof garden suddenly assumes the function that a park had in Max Kolb's time.

When it comes to inducing community in the offices below, the so-called Openhouse has a special function. This is a spacious lounge where the aspect of diversity plays just as significant a role in the furnishings as it does on the roof. Ilse Crawford sofas are paired with Vincent van Duysen chairs, and casino lights from the 1960s complement Venetian Diamond Lamps. What has found its way in here has been carefully curated. You will look in vain for cheap or even toxic plastics; the canon of materials naturally ranges from wood, leather, stone, metal, and high-quality textiles.

Companies, departments, managers, and creative people who have previously worked exclusively for themselves should feel encouraged by this level of quality to step out of isolation and enter new meeting spaces. Although a stylishly furnished conference room is also part of the lounge, overall, it does not convey the sense of urgency to work. The idea is that you can come down here, switch off and have a relaxed espresso conversation—perhaps even with someone you would never have met if you had continued to sit in your silo. The fact that the Openhouse and its roof terrace are located on the fifth floor, allowing visitors to combine their chill-out time with a view over Munich's city center, as well as the curated events that offer immaterial added value, could be another argument for leaving work a little earlier. No need for a guilty conscience, as the flower beds on the roof also encourage people to arrive at work earlier in the morning. Because fresh berries for muesli also grow there. Messrs Lenbach and Kolb would certainly have applauded this reinterpretation of modern working environments.

GRAINHOUSE
LONDON, UNITED KINGDOM
BARR GAZETAS ARCHITECTS

Anyone who decides to visit the London district of Covent Garden usually has cultural plans. Countless theaters, many pubs and restaurants, museums, and the legendary indoor market attract locals and travelers from all over the world. But right in the middle of it all, on the corner of Drury Lane and Dryden Street, just opposite a musical stage, there has also been a highlight for architecture aficionados since 2023—Grainhouse. Where, around 160 years ago, a brass and iron foundry created a lot of air, where a seed merchant opened his main warehouse in 1915, and where fashion boutiques and cafés attracted the public from 1980 onwards, today it is mainly office space. Office space? That may sound boring in contrast to the artistic surroundings. Still, the creative minds at Barr Gazetas and the developers at Hines, one of the world's leading real estate investment managers, staged it in such a way that the Grainhouse became a showpiece of New Work architecture.

However, before it could become what it is today, the big question had to be answered: how on earth can you achieve your goal in such a historic district where everything has to be handled with kid gloves? For ten years, various interested parties had been thinking about redeveloping the site. Ultimately, it was the complexity and urban context that repeatedly led to the plans being rejected. To understand the difficulty, you need to know that "Grainhouse" does not mean one building, but an entire block, or more precisely, five buildings within a block. The trick was therefore to merge these different units into a seamless whole, proving that imposing, historic buildings can be transformed into flexible, light-flooded workspaces that meet the demands of the 21st century.

This was achieved using the cut-and-carve method, gutting the entire block and preserving the façades at the same time. Inside, a steel construction was used to generously structure the complex as a whole and group the five units around a newly created atrium. To create an authentic industrial charm, a kind of warehouse romance, so to speak, concrete, light-colored brick, and wood complement the visible black metal struts. Many of the materials were salvaged from the rubble created during demolition, reused, and combined with newly manufactured components such as highly efficient building and insulation technologies. Both contribute to the building's comparatively low carbon footprint.

The 67,000 square meters of office space are spread over five floors—the building was extended by two translucent floors—and are primarily tailored to small and medium-sized companies. Real estate developer Hines, with over 5,000 employees in 31 countries, stands out due to its size alone. It has even decided to set up its European headquarters in the high-quality showpiece block, occupying three floors alone. The work and recreation areas, decorated in elegant, unagitated pastel shades, are arranged around an open stairwell. Wherever you look, plants contribute to the relaxed atmosphere. An indication that the health and well-being of the workforce was the focus of the Grainhouse concept. The richly planted roof terrace with a view over London fits in with this, as do the showers with changing rooms, which encourage people to cycle to work even over longer distances. Only on the ground floor of Grainhouse, where the streams of tourists pass by, do you not sit at a desk. In a nod to the multifunctional use of the location, the lower areas were designed for gastronomy.

GRAINHOUSE

SCHINKEL DISTRICT
AMSTERDAM, THE NETHERLANDS
JAMESTOWN AND NEXT ARCHITECTS

When a district has its own Instagram account that can easily compete with those of popular influencers in terms of energy and buzz, it's worth taking a closer look. Behind the colorful posts of spectacular architecture, creative new-work locations, unusual clothing stores, and gastro menus, well-attended yoga classes and exuberant parties, unusual works of art, or simply quietly gliding water against an autumnal tree backdrop lies the Schinkel District in the south of Amsterdam. The Schinkel name does not originate from the German architect Karl Friedrich Schinkel, as he played no role in the area's development, but rather because the river that runs through the district is called the Schinkel.

In neighborhoods like these, which have been helped into the modern age, you can immediately see that for the longest time, money was made here with other business models. Here, people worked hard. Here, they got stuck in. Here, people went home with their hands dirty. The heart of today's Schinkel District is a nearly 12,000-square-meter building complex, designed in 1955 as a bicycle factory and now known as A-Factorij. Like waves crashing into the sea, five elongated halls with rounded roofs, paying homage to Brick Brutalism, are stacked next to each other. Today, you can see in every square meter what the plan was: to breathe new life into urban communities through adaptive conversion projects, to create innovative spaces, while preserving the charm of the past. Photographers, furniture manufacturers, artists, architects, designers, as well as marketing and technology experts, have become the next generation of tenants and have transformed the former bicycle factory into an epicenter of entrepreneurial and creative change.

But not everyone here is going their own way. Previously used space has been transformed into a lounge, meeting rooms are available to everyone, shared shower facilities are available, and rooms for breastfeeding mothers are accessible to every company. The connecting elements also radiate outwards: a window facing the street has been transformed into a gallery, whose works change every six weeks.

The Helicopterstraat, which is in the immediate vicinity of the A-Factorij, will soon be just as creative. In addition to the existing modern office buildings with a total area of approximately 7,300 square meters, two interconnected warehouses (totaling 5,900 square meters) will be converted into spaces for artisans, cafés, stores, and offices. Once completed, a covered passageway—known as Makers Alley—will span the buildings, providing visitors with an insight into the production facilities. The workshops will be combined with stores, allowing makers to sell directly to customers.

The real estate investor and manager Jamestown, which, together with its joint venture partners—the RAG Foundation and the pension assets of the E.ON Group—has purchased and transformed many other production facilities around the architectural centerpiece over the years, is jointly responsible for the impetus. Like undiscovered treasures, they have been unearthed and transformed into precious elements of a larger vision, namely, in cooperation with the city of Amsterdam, to bring an entire district back to life.

Modern working practices will also be supported in the new acquisitions—but not only. The mixed use creates the vibrancy of the area. People can live there, spend their free time there, satisfy their hunger, go shopping, and do something for their health. In a few years, not only will the part of the so-called *Schinkelkwartier* for which Jamestown is responsible be in full bloom. By then, the entire harbor district between the old Olympic Stadium in the east and Schiphol Airport in the west will have been transformed in the course of a massive 25-year urban development strategy so that 22,000 people can live and 45,500 people can work there. A completely isolated working-class district will have been transformed into a green, vibrant, and inclusive neighborhood that can be easily accessed by bike and public transport—and will finally beckon to the curious: "Go on!"

PILOTENSTRAAT
VANVLIET

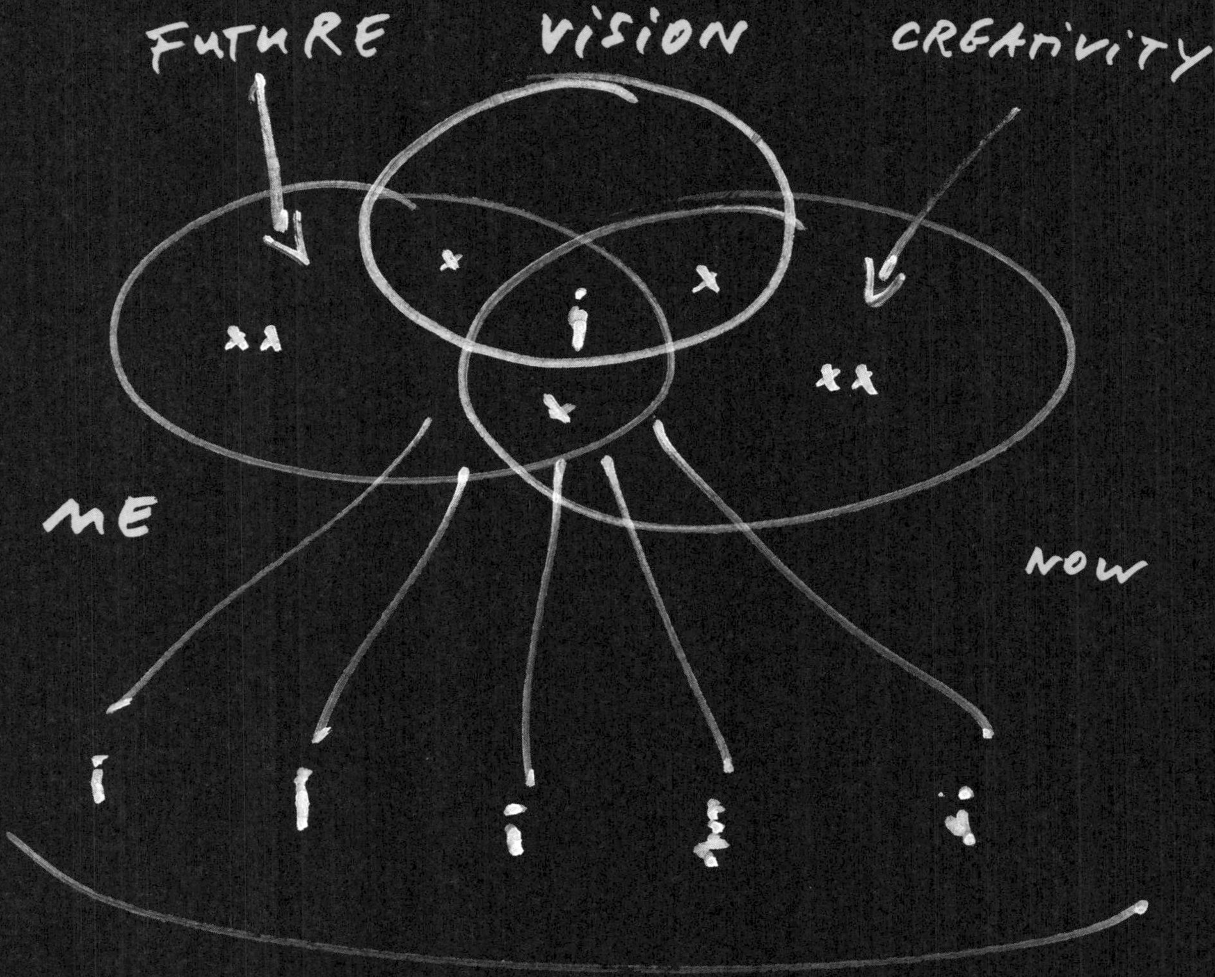
FUTURE
VISION
CREATIVITY
ME
NOW

HOUSES AS NUTRIENTS

OPEN SPACES OF COOPERATION—The places of work as we know them must become places of cooperation. Udo Schaffer is firmly convinced of this. However, this will only succeed if offices and office districts are planned, built, and designed with a sense of appreciation and if people, as their central users, finally retake center stage. Identification, pride, and creative productivity are the almost inevitable results. Schaffer provides proof of this success with the Munich *Lenbachgärten Offices*—the vision you can touch. An encounter.

The view extends far over the green roof terraces and the treetops of the Old Botanical Gardens to the colossal roof structure of the Bavarian Palace of Justice. Further south, the towers of the Frauenkirche can be seen, and to the other side, Königsplatz with the Propylaea, the Collection of Classical Antiquities, and the Glyptothek. We are in the heart of Munich. And not only that: we are in the heart of the Lenbachgärten, a quiet, green neighborhood of residential buildings, office buildings, and a hotel, just a five-minute walk from Munich Central Station.

The heart of the Lenbachgärten Offices is the Openhouse on the fifth floor of a building on Karlstrasse. From here, you not only have a 360-degree view over the rooftops of Munich's city center, but you also have the opportunity to enjoy an espresso, work in peace, gather for a meeting, or simply unwind. And all this in an attractively designed ambience that invites people to linger—not only those who work for one of the companies that has rented space in the Lenbachgärten Offices, but also people from the neighborhood, who are also welcome here. The Lenbachgärten Offices offer around 30,000 square meters of office space, but the epicenter of the quarter is the Openhouse. There can be no doubt about that.

It is therefore no coincidence that we meet Udo Schaffer here. He is one of the driving forces behind the fact that the Lenbachgärten Offices can now serve as a trailblazer for office areas in Germany. In close cooperation with real estate manager Hines and the Munich design studio Blackspace, he has been working since 2021 to bring a shared vision to life: that of a future neighborhood. The Openhouse, where we meet Udo Schaffer, makes this vision tangible: he is convinced that offices of the future will increasingly become places of human encounters, places of togetherness, where people are at the center and employees can develop their potential. "One person alone," he says, "cannot grow. It always needs others; it needs encounters. It requires cooperation and co-creativity." The space that needs to be created for this purpose should be "a greenhouse for people," "a space in which they feel comfortable, in which they can think ahead together without fear and grow together."

This vision aligns perfectly with an area that already has "garden" in its name. The Lenbachgärten Offices seem tailor-made to be an innovation space and future laboratory for the working worlds of the future: for new offices that are no longer designed according to sterile value creation machines but are transformed into cultural spaces for the development of human and economic potential. There is much to suggest that such a paradigm shift in work is already underway, at least since the COVID-19 pandemic, when large parts of office work were moved to employees' homes. Quite a few of them have noticed that they sometimes work more effectively and with greater concentration from home than in their companies' offices. The consequence is obvious: sooner or later, they have to ask themselves why they should stop working from home at all. Especially now that they no longer lose valuable time commuting and can organize their working hours more flexibly. The work-life balance demanded by many young employees was also much easier to manage while working from home than with eight-hour days in the company office plus travel times. Why do without it? It's no wonder that the traditional office was declared dead by many entrepreneurs and architects following COVID-19.

Udo Schaffer sees it differently. "Nobody can break the office up," he is convinced. He admits that it "certainly makes sense for people to work from home more often, especially when they are completing tasks that require their full concentration." However, from what we know, the "efficiency of work is higher when people are physically together," especially as this is precisely what many people crave.

We want to know from Udo Schaffer whether he has an explanation for this. His answer convinces us. "The quality of experience plays a central role for the new generation," he says, "nobody wants to work in an office building with individual offices and a glass tower over five floors anymore." The workplace where someone sits at the same desk all day no longer exists. "Work has become more flexible. We can respond to this by creating more space for people to meet, providing common areas outside the offices, and repurposing space." Closing offices and cutting back on workspaces, therefore, does not seem to be the right approach: "We don't need *less* space in the offices, but *different* spaces, no more isolated offices, but open spaces for collaboration, no more narrow desks, but wide project spaces." These are the pillars of what is being discussed today under the heading of "people-centered work." However, Udo Schaffer also knows that many investors do not want or cannot afford something like this, which ultimately prevents these processes from taking place. In his opinion, they have then "made savings in the wrong places." Because "if you want to be sustainably successful as an investor, you have to think outside the box and break new ground." Today, this means, above all, asking what needs to be done "so that in the future a place of work can become a place of collaboration."

In Udo Schaffer's eyes, such future-oriented thinking is not witchcraft. He knows that it is often possible to change the entire appearance of a working environment with relatively little effort. Even details can make a decisive difference and build appreciation for the workplace. "People should only work in buildings that they can be proud of and identify with." That is what matters, and that is what he intends to do with the Lenbachgärten Offices, "to create spaces in which people feel comfortable, in which they are proud—spaces like this one." With that, Udo Schaffer draws our attention back to where we are right now: the Openhouse, the day bar on the fifth floor.

In the meantime, we have a coffee in front of us, with only the large windows separating us from the green roof terraces of the area. Indeed, a place to feel good and certainly a place that addresses the lifestyle of today's office workers. Udo Schaffer feels the same way. "You go here to be with people," he explains, "or to work in a different atmosphere. In the summer, you sit on the terrace, in the winter in comfortable armchairs. People appreciate that." The fact that the Openhouse at the Lenbachgärten Offices is so popular is primarily due to the colleagues at the Blackspace agency, who developed the space. In particular, the designer Sarah-Joan Fuld deserves a mention, as she created the incomparable interior of this lounge with great love and intuition. It is also thanks to her that you, dear readers, are holding this book in your hands. Originally planned as a literary work about the Lenbachgärten, it evolved into much more during the course of the project: a fundamental statement about the power of innovative office spaces.

In her own words, designer Sarah-Joan Fuld tells us what she had in mind for the Lenbachgärten: "I wanted to create a place where you can clear your head and feel at home. The things here are not loud, but they speak. I believe that people also feel with their eyes. They see, and without knowing it, this perception influences their feelings and thoughts." And she emphasizes: "It is my deep conviction that spaces and things that are in a harmonious context are good for people. And so design has the task of creating the right setting for the different moments in life." There is no doubt that she has succeeded in this endeavor with the Lenbachgärten Offices Openhouse. That can already be said, even if the full potential of this space has yet to be realized. In any event, Udo Schaffer and his team have big plans for it. In the future, there will be events for the tenants here, such as lectures, fireside chats, or other activities that support their creative interaction.

The sophisticated and loving design of the Openhouse should be seen against this background. According to the real estate developer, the most important thing for him is to create an atmosphere that allows the people working there to feel comfortable. High-quality design and artistic architecture are the necessary prerequisites for this, but they should not become an end in themselves. In the end, the aesthetics must be coordinated with the use, because despite all the beauty, one must never lose sight of the fact that the buildings have to earn money, which is only possible if they are also highly functional.

Another point is important to our interviewee. A high-quality design, such as that of the Lenbachgärten Offices, he says, does not suit every building and does not fit into every environment. However, the latter in particular plays a not insignificant role in the design of office areas. When planning the Lenbachgärten Offices, it was therefore crucial for him, and everyone involved in the project, to integrate the quarter harmoniously into its surroundings and to open it up to the people in the neighborhood. It is therefore not only the Openhouse that is open to external guests. An educational herb trail on the roofs is also being planned, which could be visited by school classes from the surrounding area in the future. Alternatively, there is the idea of creating small planting beds for neighbors who do not have their own garden. This social vision has been around for a long time, but approval is proving difficult.

Udo Schaffer also considers the participation of residents in the surrounding area to be necessary from an investor's point of view, because "whether a property is successful in the long term or not also depends on real involvement in its surroundings." Schaffer also expects tenants to benefit considerably from the neighborhood projects he has outlined. "Being close to nature creates an atmosphere that is not only beneficial, but also supports creative processes," he says, recalling the ancient construction methods that are still common in the Mediterranean region today, which placed great value on integrating nature into people's living space in the atrium and patio. In the Lenbachgärten Offices, this will primarily take place on the green roof areas. They will lend the quarter a unique atmosphere of liveliness and creativity, so that it can be described as more than just a metaphorical greenhouse. In fact, it will also exude the fresh impression of a garden.

Incidentally, this also applies to the constellation of tenants who have already made their home here. Just as in a beautiful and well-designed garden, where different plants fertilize

each other, Udo Schaffer would like to see fruitful interaction within the neighborhood at Lenbachgärten Offices. After all, it will only function as a "thriving greenhouse" if the tenants are willing to "use the existing network areas and engage in exchange, talk to each other, perhaps even rub up against each other." Only then will inspiration and motivation germinate—the most important nutrients to stay in the picture. But that's not all. The leitmotif of the greenhouse inspires Schaffer to make another comparison. Offices of the future, hepredicts, will be "open office landscapes," "interspersed with many glazed project rooms that create an atmosphere of activity." He would like to see this above all because, in his experience, it is energizing to witness how colleagues work together with commitment in such a "greenhouse."

Udo Schaffer describes the reception area as the first point of contact: "a mixed gastronomic landscape without any canteen flair that exudes the spirit of variety and diversity. I find inviting seating areas where people can retreat to work. Some alone, others in groups. I would like to see in-house services, such as IT, located on the first floor in open, shop-like spaces. The building should be sustainable and have good public transport connections." This is how he completes his visionary show. He lets his gaze wander over the rooftops ofMunich and becomes humble and modest despite his justified pride. "We're not the only ones working on this," says Udo Schaffer, and tells us about a whole series of innovative projects around the world that are pursuing similar visions.

The last thing we want to know from him is whether he will continue to realize such buildings in the near future. "There will be such buildings," is his answer, "but I'm not the one who brings them to life. I help design them a little, share my experiences and visions with our local partners. They are always the smarter ones. They possess the concepts and the workforce to bring the jointly developed visions from concept to reality. To me, this is a lifelong learning process. And I think that's wonderful."

JAN TEUNEN
Cultural Capital Producer

CHRISTOPH QUARCH
Philosopher

MARTIN HÄUSLER
Journalist and Author

UDO SCHAFFER
Head of Real Estate E.ON SE

SARAH-JOAN FULD
Architectural Designer

MICHAEL KELLER
Designer

MORITZ FUHRMANN
Designer

MANFRED JARISCH
Photographer

FRANÇOIS TRAUSCH
CEO and Chief Investment Officer
at PIMCO Prime Real Estate

MICHELE DE LUCCHI
Architect, Designer, and Artist

ROBERT THIEMANN
Journalist and Author,
Founder of *Frame* Magazine and Betterness

DORINE DE VOS
Art Director, Project Developer,
Illustrator, and Artist

HANS ULRICH OBRIST
Author, Curator, and Artistic Director
of the Serpentine Galleries, London

ANDREW TUCK
Co-Founder and Editor-in-Chief
of the Global Magazine *Monocle*

MICHAEL PHILLIPS
President of the US
Real Estate Company Jamestown

ROB SPEYER
CEO of Tishman Speyer

LAURA HINES-PIERCE
Co-CEO at Hines Global Real Estate

LUCA BALLARINI
Founder and Director of Stratosferica

ENDNOTES

1 cf. www.gallup.com/de/472028/bericht-zum-engagement-index-deutschland.aspx (Accessed July 31, 2024)

2 cf. www.statista.com/statistik/daten/studie/1290347/umfrage/geschaeftsrisiken-fuer-die-deutsche-industrie/ (Accessed July 31, 2024)

3 According to the *lidA—Leben in der Arbeit* study conducted by the University of Wuppertal, around 68% of respondents at the beginning of 2024 planned to retire early. cf. www.businessinsider.de/leben/immer-mehr-menschen-gehen-frueher-in-rente-aber-das-nicht-immer-freiwillig/ (Accessed July 31, 2024)

4 cf. www.marconomy.de/das-sind-die-top-10-erwartungen-an-den-neuen-arbeitgeber-a-501760/ (Accessed July 31, 2024)

5 Hesiod: Theogony 116, in the translation from Glenn W. Most: Hesiod, Theogony, Works and Days, Testimonia, Cambridge, MA 2006, p. 13.

6 The Homeric Hymns: XXX—Hymn to Gaia, Mother of All in the translation from Jules Cashford: The Homeric Hymns, London 2003, p. 140.

7 René Descartes: Discours de la Méthode (Discourse on Methold) in the translation from Arthur Wollaston, London 1960, p. 84.

8 cf. Vitruv: Zehn Bücher über Architektur, transl. and ed. by Curt Fensterbusch, Darmstadt 1987. Especially the chapters 2.1.1. through 2.1.7., p. 79-85.

9 Ibid., chapter 2.1.6, p. 83

10 Hans von Trotha: Im Garten der Romantik, Berlin 2016, p. 14.

11 Friedrich Schiller: Ueber den Gartenkalender auf das Jahr 1795, www.projekt-gutenberg.org/schiller/gartenk/gartenk.html

12 Giovanni Boccaccio: The Decameron, vol. 1, translated by J. M. Rigg, London 1930, p. 176.

13 For more information, refer to a chapter below, "The house. Remembrance" paragraph 5.

14 Dostoyevsky: Fyodor Dostoyevsky: The Idiot, in the translation from Constance Garnett, New York 1970, p. 423.

15 Buckminster Fuller: R. Buckminster Fuller, Your Private Sky, the Art of Design Science. Ed. Joachim Krausse and Claude Lichtenstein, Zurich 2017.

16 Clive Wilkinson: Clive Wilkinson, The Theatre of Work, Ed. Frame Publishers, 2019.

17 R. Tagore: Rabindranath Tagore, Selected Essays. New Delhi 2004, p. 97.

18 Édouard Glissant, Penseur des archipels (AGORA t.365) (French Edition)

19 Norman Potter: What Is a Designer: Things, Places, Messages Hyphen Press, 2002

20 Sir Patrick Geddes (1854–1932) was a Scottish biologist, geographer, and botanist. He is known as an innovative thinker in the field of urban planning.

IMAGE CREDITS

THE GREENHOUSE
P. 13–47 Myrzik and Jarisch

WISDOM AND FORESIGHT
P. 66–195 Myrzik and Jarisch

LEARNING FROM GARDENS
P. 217–225 Jason Ingram

NEIGHBORHOODS FOR THE FUTURE
P. 233–239 Hiroyuki Oki
P. 241 Takuji Shimmura
P. 243 Vincent Leroux
P. 244–245 Takuji Shimmura
P. 247–251 Jamestown
P. 252–253 S9 Architecture, Garey Gomez
P. 255–263 Stratosferica
P. 265 Bloomimages
P. 268–269 Moka Studios
P. 270 Snøhetta
P. 271 Moka Studios
P. 281–283 Giacomo Albo
P. 284–285 Carola Merello
P. 286–287 Giacomo Albo
P. 289–295 Myrzik and Jarisch
P. 297 Philip Vile
P. 299–302 Piranha
P. 303 Philip Vile
P. 305–310 Jamestown Europe/
Photographed by Marcel IJzerman

HOUSES AS NUTRIENTS
P. 316–328 Myrzik and Jarisch

PROJECT PARTICIPANTS
P. 333 Andra
P. 333Daniel Nicolas
P. 333 Elias Hassos
P. 333 Federico Masini
P. 333 Hines
P. 333 Martin Grothmaak
P. 333 Martin Kreuzer
P. 333 Myrzik and Jarisch
P. 333 Myrzik and Jarisch
P. 333 Myrzik and Jarisch
P. 333 Myrzik and Jarisch
P. 333 PIMCO Prime Real Estate
P. 333 Sasha Maslov
P. 333 Stefan Blume
P. 333 Courtesy of Tishman Speyer
P. 333 Trisha Ward
P. 333 Ulrich Mayer

IMPRINT

The German National Library lists this publication in the German National Bibliography; detailed bibliographic data is available on the Internet at http://dnb.dnb.de.

ISBN 978-3-7212-1054-5

www.braun-publishing.ch

First Edition 2025

Product Security
Publisher: Braun Publishing AG
Arenenbergstr. 2, 8268 Salenstein, Switzerland
publisher@braun-publishing.ch
EU-Representative: Bookwise GmbH
Zeppelinstr. 67, 81669 Munich, Germany
info@bookwise.de

CONCEPT AND CURATION
Sarah-Joan Fuld, Jan Teunen

AUTHORS
Jan Teunen, Christoph Quarch, Martin Häusler

CREATIVE DIRECTION
Moritz Fuhrmann, Michael Keller, Blackspace

ART DIRECTION
Magdalena Stricker, Blackspace

ORGANIZATION AND PROJECT MANAGEMENT
Sarah-Joan Fuld, Alexandra von Prittwitz, Blackspace

ILLUSTRATION
Michael Keller

PROOFREADING
Martin Häusler

TRANSLATION
Dan Reynolds

PHOTOGRAPHY
Myrzik and Jarisch

EDITOR
Sarah-Joan Fuld, Blackspace

PAPER
Munken Lynx Rough 115g

TYPEFACE
LD Grotesk

PUBLISHER
Niggli

For Pepe, Oscar, and their generation, so that we leave them a world that thrives and breathes.

INITIATORS

JAN TEUNEN
Cultural Capital Producer
"I am convinced that beauty is a responsible response to the crises of the present. It will lead us gently into the future."

CHRISTOPH QUARCH
Philosopher
"What is there to do? Opening spaces for the spirit, finding words for the spirit, paving the way for the spirit."

MARTIN HÄUSLER
Journalist and Author
"We can trust no one but nature."

UDO SCHAFFER
Head of Real Estate E.ON SE
"I love to see how the (real estate) world is constantly changing so that I always have to question my own convictions."

SARAH-JOAN FULD
Architectural Designer
"It's quite simple: good people—good projects."